Also by Keith Clouten

Reid's Mistake: A History of Lake Macquarie to 1890

Hunter Valley Bush Walk

Journeys: Devotions for Travelers

The Road from Stoney Creek: a Personal Journey

*Breaking Through the Wall:
How God Communicates With His Lost Creation*

A Day for Joy

Experiencing the Sabbath Day

Keith Clouten

Energion Publications
Gonzalez, Florida
2022

Copyright © 2022, Keith Clouten

Scripture quotations marked (NLT) are taken from the Holy Bible, New Living Translation, copyright ©1996, 2004, 2015 by Tyndale House Foundation. Used by permission of Tyndale House Publishers, Carol Stream, Illinois 60188. All rights reserved.

Scripture quotations marked (NIV) are taken from the Holy Bible, New International Version®, NIV®. Copyright © 1973, 1978, 1984, 2011 by Biblica, Inc.™ Used by permission of Zondervan. All rights reserved worldwide. www.zondervan.com The "NIV" and "New International Version" are trademarks registered in the United States Patent and Trademark Office by Biblica, Inc.™

Scripture quotations marked (TNIV) Scripture taken from the HOLY BIBLE, TODAY'S NEW INTERNATIONAL VERSION®. Copyright © 2001, 2005 by Biblica®. Used by permission of Biblica®. All rights reserved worldwide.

Scripture quotations marked (NKJV) are taken from the New King James Version®. Copyright © 1982 by Thomas Nelson. Used by permission. All rights reserved.

Scripture quotations marked (NRSV) are taken from New Revised Standard Version Bible, copyright © 1989 National Council of the Churches of Christ in the United States of America. Used by permission. All rights reserved worldwide.

Scripture quotations marked (NASB) are taken from the NEW AMERICAN STANDARD BIBLE(R), Copyright (C) 1960,1962,1963,1968,1971,1972,1973 ,1975,1977,1995 by The Lockman Foundation. Used by permission.

Scripture quotations marked (NCV) are taken from the New Century Version®. Copyright © 2005 by Thomas Nelson. Used by permission. All rights reserved.

Scripture quotations marked (NEB) are taken from the New English Bible, copyright © Cambridge University Press and Oxford University Press 1961, 1970. All rights reserved.

ISBN: 978-1-63199-804-1
eISBN: 978-1-63199-805-8

Energion Publications
PO Box 841
Gonzalez, FL 32560
https://energion.com
pubs@energion.com

Editor's Foreword

This book is written by a Seventh Day Adventist from a conventional SDA interpretational stance, and SDA and Conservative and Evangelical readers are unlikely to have any difficulty with this and can go straight to the text. Readers who adopt a more liberal or progressive reading of scripture will, however, probably have some issues, particularly with the argument in Chapter 2.

I would invite these readers to pause for a moment and consider that a large amount of what we read or watch is not, in fact, actual events, but stories - and the merit of a story is often not found in whether it's a faithful account of how things actually happened, but in how it makes us think and feel. Jesus regularly used story (for example the Good Samaritan) to prompt his audience to think, and the effect of that story is completely independent of whether there actually were a man set on by robbers, a priest, a Levite and a Samaritan who did as Jesus recounted. Indeed, stopping to ask whether they did actually exist and act as the parable states is counterproductive. There is, I understand, a tradition among some African story-tellers of starting off their account by saying "I don't know if it happened this way, but I know this story is true".

The editor is a liberal-to-radical theologian and therefore considers it very unlikely that the account in Genesis 1 to 3 "happened like that" - but he knows "that story is true", and knows that the author's love of the Sabbath and Sabbath-keeping shines brightly through this narrative. Try to read this book in that spirit...

Chris Eyre

Acknowledgements

I'm grateful to several people who have been critical listeners or meticulous readers: Don Corkum, our family pastor who welcomed us to Canada; Ron Sydenham, a pastor of our College Heights Church and a spiritual encourager; Denis Fortin, whose scholarship and writings always bless me; Wendy Jackson, New Zealander, family friend, and religion professor at Avondale University in Australia; Henry Neufeld, my generous, open-hearted publisher; and Chris Eyre, my discriminating editor and risk-taker with an Adventist manuscript.

Keith Clouten

WHY SABBATH?

What does "Sabbath" mean to you?
Late one Friday afternoon I was walking through the crowded market alleys of Old Jerusalem on my way to the famous Western Wall. The streets were busy and noisy as customers haggled with food vendors vigorously selling and clearing their stalls. Later that evening, as I headed back the way I had come, the dimly lit alleyways were silent and empty, the stalls shuttered. Sabbath had arrived in Jerusalem.

Traditionally, Sabbath is a festive day for Jews the world over. According to their religious law, Sabbath is observed from a few minutes before sunset on Friday until the appearance of three stars in the sky on Saturday evening. Sabbath for them is a time of joyful fellowship, ushered in with lighting of candles and closed with a special blessing. One renowned Jewish scholar, Abraham Heschel, greets Sabbath as "a palace in time."

Christians inherited their Sabbath from the Jews, but in a reaction to Jewishness, the early Christian church moved worship from Saturday to Sunday, honoring Jesus' resurrection. Today, Christianity maintains its place as the world's dominant religion, though Islam has been doing a catch-up. In the Western World, though, most Christian churches are experiencing a decline in membership and Sunday worship attendance. In America, the Pew Research Center reports a rapid decline in membership among Protestant churches since the beginning of this century.[1]

---

[1] Pew Research Center: *Religion and Public Life*. Report dated 17 October, 2019.

A similar trend is seen in Catholic worship. In his 2018 annual address in St. Peter's Square in Rome, Pope Francis deplored the loss of spiritual commitment among followers due to secularism. "The dominant concept of life today does not have its center of gravity in commitment, but in evasion," he said, adding, "Man has never experienced so much emptiness as today."[2]

Pope Francis remarked on lifestyle "emptiness". Brushing aside the religious viewpoint, humanity's need for a regular time of rest is apparent in our fragmented world. It is frightening that in Canada and the United States a growing number of young people are choosing death instead of life. Suicide speaks to meaninglessness and loss of hope in a world characterized by social unrest, political turmoil, mental and emotional distress, divorce, and financial insecurity. The weekly Sabbath is intended to bring meaning and hope. For the one experiencing stress and mental exhaustion, Sabbath may bring quiet and healing. For the lonely it offers community in a fellowship of faith.

Our Jewish friends have historically valued their Sabbath for the meaning it gives to the earth and their identity as a people. In a recent article, Jonathan Schorsch argues for Sabbath in an era of climate change. Imagine, he says, if we each consistently chose one day out of seven to essentially eliminate our own harm to the environment. "Sabbath properly practiced offers a weekly interruption of the suicidal econometric fantasy of infinite growth, a weekly divestment from fossil fuels, a weekly investment in local community." He concludes: "This means that if you belong to a group or people that practices a day of rest, for the sake of our planetary health, you will make that day as free as possible from any manipulation of nature."[3]

---

2 "Pope Francis speaks of rest: Sunday is the day of thanksgiving for the gift of life" (youtube, uploaded by *Rome Reports* in English, September 5, 2018.)

3 Jonathan Schorsch, "The Sabbath in an Era of Climate Change", *Tablet Magazine*, 3 February, 2020.

The earliest Christian approach to Sabbath and Sunday observance was strictly law-based. Sabbath rest was not only expected, but demanded. God's Ten Commandments were accepted as the moral foundation of society. That included "Remember the Sabbath Day to keep it holy." In the intervening two millennia most of that emphasis on law has dissipated.

On one occasion, I was sitting in the departure lounge at San Juan airport in Puerto Rico. While waiting for my flight to be called, I fell into conversation with a Christian gentleman from Grand Rapids, Michigan. He worked in the editorial department of an evangelical publishing company. I had recently submitted a manuscript of devotional readings to a west coast publisher. We chatted about Christian publishing and some common points of our faith before he said, "It's too bad that Seventh-day Adventists are stuck in the Old Testament with their law-keeping." I knew he was thinking about the Adventist emphasis on the fourth commandment. I responded by telling him that my Sabbath-keeping had nothing to do with earning my salvation, which depended entirely on my faith in Christ's death on the cross for me.

Which brings the question: If I am not saved by my Sabbath-keeping, why do I observe it? Does it really matter which day I choose to worship my God? In the fourth commandment of Exodus, God specifies his authority as the Creator of everything. So, is obedience the sole reason for my Sabbath-keeping? My airport friend from Grand Rapids probably thinks it is.

As I reflect on that airport conversation, I have to admit that my Sabbath-keeping is too often a "doing" thing, a "law-keeping" assignment. I grew up with all sorts of rules that governed my Sabbath worship. If I wanted to go to heaven someday, I knew I must keep the seventh day holy as God had commanded. Most of my friends at church and school believed the same thing. As my faith matured, however, I wanted my Sabbath-keeping to be a joyful love response to my Lord and Savior, yet I continued to take pride in my obedience to God's fourth commandment.

Is Sabbath-keeping relevant in the 21st century? If it is, how can Sabbath observance be more about "experiencing" than "doing"? This small book is an attempt to answer that question. Have we mined the depths of meaning in the day we keep holy? Several Christian writers have delved into that question; some of them are Sunday-keepers who have contributed much to my thinking on the topic. You may look for their names in my bibliography.

Whether you worship on Saturday or Sunday—or on any other day of the week for that matter—I invite you to join me as we explore together how Sabbath gives meaning to our existence on this planet.

Keith Clouten

Table of Contents

  Editor's Foreword iii
  Acknowledgements v
  Why Sabbath? vii

1 Lord of the Sabbath 1
2 Creation and Sabbath 5

A Day for Rest

3 Time to Rest 13
4 Rest in Another Dimension 19
5 Rest for the Oppressed 25

A Day for Relationship

6 Hand Made 31
7 Designed by God 37
8 The Gifted Earth 43

A Day for Redemption

9 The Covenant 51
10 The Promise 57
11 The Fulfillment 63

Recession

12	Sabbath in Recession	71
13	Creation in Pain	79

Restoration

14	Sabbath Restoration	87
15	Sabbath-Keeping	91
16	Home-Coming	97
	My Takeaways	99
	Sabbath: A Select Bibliography	101

1

LORD OF THE SABBATH

It happened one Sabbath day near the lakeside town of Capernaum in northern Galilee. Jesus and his disciples were wending their way through a grain field, their every movement watched by some religious activists known as Pharisees. Mark, the gospel writer, picks up the story: "One Sabbath day as Jesus was walking through some grain fields, his disciples began breaking off heads of grain to eat. But the Pharisees said to Jesus, 'Look, why are they breaking the law by harvesting grain on the Sabbath?'" (Mark 2:23 NLT).

Was this a problem? The unthinking unsuspecting wayfarers were not stealing or spoiling the crop. Just plucking a few ears of wheat or barley as they made their way through the field. On any other day of the week nobody would have raised a hair. But in the eyes of the Sabbath police, the disciples were not only plucking, which was akin to harvesting, but also threshing and grinding the grain in the palms of their hands. They were flouting several Sabbath regulations.

Jesus responded to the question with one of his own: "Haven't you ever read in the Scriptures what David did when he and his companions were hungry? He went into the house of God . . . and broke the law by eating the sacred loaves of bread that only the priests are allowed to eat" (Mark 2:24-26 NLT).

Oops. Of course they had read that story as recorded in the Book of Samuel (1 Sam 21:6). Pharisees prided themselves in their knowledge of the Scriptures and especially their guardianship of the law. What David did long ago, when he was a fugitive from the army of King Saul, was an embarrassment to them. So, they did not respond to Jesus' question.

But the itinerant teacher had something to say, and his words shocked them. "*The Sabbath was made for people, and not people for the Sabbath. The Son of Man is even Lord of the Sabbath*" (Mark 2:27,28 TNIV). Those were words of authority.

Jesus' words undermined the Pharisees' claim to be the guardians of the Sabbath. Mind you, their motives were beyond reproach. For centuries Pharisees had led their people in interpreting and obeying the Scriptures. To protect the Sabbath from neglect and disobedience, they had instituted a bundle of rules for its observance. They were the arbiters of Sabbath behavior.

By saying he was "Lord of the Sabbath", Jesus was informing the Pharisees and the disciples that he held *ownership* of the Sabbath because he had divinely *instituted* it at creation. It was in every sense *his* day. He made and designed the Sabbath with a purpose that was totally at odds with the warped concept of the rule-makers. Sabbath was created to be a day of joy—a celebration of the finished work of creation. "Sabbath is about life, not rules, though rules are appropriate when they help us to enjoy the Sabbath."[4] Jesus was a faithful Sabbath-keeper: "As his custom was, he went into the synagogue on the Sabbath day" (Luke 4:16 NKJV).

Jesus' authority was firmly based on his claim to be the earth's creator. The Scriptures confirm that he was indeed the one who created and sustains all life. Study these New Testament statements:

o "He [Christ] is the image of the invisible God, the firstborn over all creation. For *by him all things were created that are in heaven and that are on earth*, visible and invisible, whether thrones or dominions or principalities or powers. *All things were created through him and for him.* And he is before all things, and in him all things consist" (Col 1:15-17 NKJV).

o "Jesus Christ, *through whom all things came* and through whom we live" (1 Cor 8:6 TNIV).

---

4   Denis Fortin, professor of historical theology at Andrews University, shared these words with me in a letter.

- "In the beginning was the Word, and the Word was with God, and the Word was God. He was with God in the beginning. *Through him all things were made; without Him nothing was made that has been made.* In him was life, and that life was the light of all people. . . He was in the world, and *though the world was made through him, the world did not recognize him*" (John 1:1-4,10 TNIV).
- "In the past God spoke to our ancestors through the prophets at many times and in various ways, but in these last days he has spoken to us by his Son, whom he appointed heir of all things, and *through whom also he made the universe*" (Heb 1:1,2 TNIV).

"Doing Good" on Sabbath

Matthew's gospel records the same story about that Sabbath walk through the grainfields and Christ's encounter with the Pharisees (Matt 12:1-8). Matthew goes on to describe something else that occurred the same day and which also affirmed Jesus' lordship of the Sabbath:

"Going on from that place, he went into their synagogue, and a man with a shriveled hand was there. Looking for a reason to accuse Jesus, they asked him, 'Is it lawful to heal on the Sabbath?'

"He said to them, 'If any of you has a sheep and it falls into a pit on the Sabbath, will you not take hold of it and lift it out? How much more valuable is a human being than a sheep! Therefore *it is lawful to do good on the Sabbath.*'

"Then he said to the man, 'Stretch out your hand.' So he stretched it out and it was completely restored, just as sound as the other. But the Pharisees went out and plotted how they might kill Jesus" (Matt 12:9-14 TNIV).

Several years ago, our family lived in a community where a Friday night storm brought a flash flood that inundated several houses in the neighborhood. On Sabbath afternoon, after attending church that morning, we and other believers strolled along the street to witness the flood damage. As we passed one of the homes, I recognized our church head elder, in overalls, shoveling mud out of someone's front door. I was surprised and shocked. Why? Was it because the elder appeared to be breaking the Sabbath? Or did I feel shame that I was not there helping with my shovel too? What did Jesus mean when he said, "it is lawful to *do good* on the Sabbath"? Think about it.

"We must view the Sabbath in all its facets as they are centered in Jesus Christ. He is not only Creator, Redeemer, and Restorer, . . . He is Lord of the Sabbath, and furthermore, he is what the Sabbath is all about."[5]

My Takeaway: *Jesus affirmed Sabbath as a time to share joy and kindness.*

Your Takeaway?

---

5   Sakae Kubo, *God Meets Man: A Theology of the Sabbath and Second Advent.* (Nashville, TN: Southern Publishing Association, 1978), 8,9.

2

CREATION AND SABBATH

When Jesus proclaimed his ownership of the Sabbath as its creator—confirmed by New Testament writers—he did not tell us when and how he did it. During a dispute with some Pharisees about divorce laws, he quoted directly from the first two chapters of Genesis: "But *at the beginning* of creation, God made them male and female. For this reason a man will leave his father and mother and be united to his wife, and the two will become one flesh." (Mark 10:6-8 TNIV; Gen 1:27, 2:24). He also acknowledged that human suffering had its origin "*from the beginning*, when God created the world, until now" (Mark 13:19 TNIV).

But when was the "beginning"? Our knowledge of the universe seems incompatible with belief in a young earth. Bishop Usher's traditional timeline of six thousand years since the creation is no longer tenable. Uncertainties about a "beginning" have produced a rash of creation scenarios that include "young" and "old" earth creationism, the gap theory, long "days" of creation, "intelligent design", and theistic evolution. We must accept, though, that the roots of our Christianity are sunk deeply in the Old Testament religion of Judaism with its central concept of a divine creation. We find allusions to creation embedded in the Scriptures all the way from Genesis to Revelation, yet we hold a variety of perceptions about creation and science and how we should relate to what is recorded in the Bible.

Among scientists who see evidence of a divine creator is Gerald Schroeder. He is an Orthodox Jew, educated in America, now living with his family in Jerusalem. Schroeder did his doctoral work at Massachusetts Institute of Technology (MIT) in the fields of nuclear physics and earth sciences, and served for a while as a member of the U.S. Atomic Energy Commission. He writes, "In the wonders of nature, we have discovered the imprint of the metaphysical within the physical. As one who sees the wake of a boat that has passed by, so we encounter the hidden face of God."[6] Although we weren't around when the boat sped by, we may get some clues by observing the ripples.

All Christians accept some things—God, for example—without scientific evidence. Yet our personal faith demands a "resting place", to use words from an old hymn, and individually, our faith has different resting points. My faith is grounded in the biblical account of a recent six-day creation of life, however and whenever it happened. Having said that, I need to be tolerant and accepting of other Bible students as we search for truth together. I need to place my trust in the one who created, looking beyond the "how" to the "why", tracing God's ultimate purposes through his Word.

EARLY CREATION ACCOUNTS

There are many ancient accounts of creation. Two of the earliest surviving pieces of literature come from ancient Babylonia. One is a collection of seven clay tablets known as "Enuma Elish" or "The Seven Tablets of Creation." They were discovered in 1849 among the ruins of ancient Nineveh and describe creation as a battle between gods. The other famous literary work is the "Epic of Gilgamesh", also recorded on clay tablets. This mythical narrative has some counterparts to the biblical story of Genesis, including a garden and a flood. The ancient Egyptians also had a creation myth in which the sun god made the earth out of chaos.

---

6 Gerald L. Schroeder, *The Hidden Face of God*. (New York: Simon & Schuster, 2001), 184.

Creation myths exist in almost every culture. The clan of Nakhi people, inhabiting the foothills of the Himalayas in the Yunnan province of China, have a creation story. During a visit there, I listened to a local shaman reading from their most famous text, a creation account. In the beginning there were seven brothers and five sisters. The gods were displeased when five of the brothers married their sisters, so they sent a great flood to destroy everyone. The two brothers who did not marry were saved from the flood by a dragon and given wives by the gods. The Nakhi descended from one brother, the Tibetans from the other.

Where did such stories originate? Is there a common source? Given the almost universal Christian belief that the Holy Scriptures are God's revelation of his activity in human history, I think it makes sense to believe that the biblical creation story is the original and authentic one. Moses, who is regarded by both Jews and Christians as the greatest of the Old Testament prophets, describes how God handed him ten commandments engraved on stone tablets (Exod 31:18; 32:15,16). The fourth of those commandments stated that "in six days the Lord made the heavens and the earth, the sea, and all that is in them, but he rested on the seventh day. Therefore the Lord blessed the Sabbath day and made it holy" (Exod 20:11 TNIV). The Genesis account of creation is unique and beautiful as we watch the six-day construction of a perfect habitat for humanity.

Looking closely at the Genesis account, we find Moses describing how God created the living earth in six literal days, yet it is recorded as a seven-day event. Our Bibles split the first two chapters of Genesis in the wrong place, which should not surprise us because the original Hebrew text did not have chapters and verses. The chronological account of creation occupies all of chapter one (days one through six) and continues into the first three verses of chapter two (day seven). Chapter two rightfully begins at verse 4 with "the account of the heavens and the earth when they were created" and it goes on to describe in detail what happened on day six—how Adam and Eve were formed and placed in a garden.

Although God finished his work on day six, there was something else he intended to do. "By *the seventh day* God had finished the work he had been doing; so on *the seventh day* he rested from all his work. Then God blessed *the seventh day* and made it holy, because on it he rested from all the work of creating that he had done" (Gen 2:2,3 TNIV). Why did he celebrate his completed creation with a holy day? Was it for himself? Surely his resting was not because of physical weariness. God likely had his newly formed human creatures in mind by establishing a "sabbath" for them.

Unfortunately for us, the Genesis account is wrapped in an ancient language and culture, and an ancient cosmology. We should not read the text of Genesis as if it has modern science embedded in it. Being aware of that, Christian thinkers speculate on widely different creation scenarios. One that is consistent with a six-day-creation has been proposed by John Walton, an eminent and respected Old Testament scholar.[7] He explains that in our culture, to create is to *make* something—a material object like a chair or a computer. Walton provides evidence that peoples of the ancient Near East did not understand the verb "create" that way. To them it meant *giving a function* to something that may have already existed—just as a computer does not become a *functional* entity until programs are installed.[8]

Walton sees creation week as God establishing *functions*—periods of light, space for life, environment—on days one to three; and *functionaries*—sun and moon for light and seasons, birds, creatures, and people for reproduction—on days four to six. The people he installs on day six have multiple roles or functions.

ORIGIN OF THE WEEK

Let us think about the origin of our week. The calendar year is defined by the earth's movement around the sun, the month

---

7 John H. Walton is Old Testament editor of the *Cultural Backgrounds Study Bible* (Grand Rapids, MI: Zondervan, 2016).
8 Walton, *The Lost World of Genesis One*. (Downers Grove, IL: IVP Academic, 2009).

A Day for Joy

by the moon's trip around the earth, but there is no astronomical explanation for the week. How and where did it originate?

'Seven' is a significant number in both the Old and New Testaments. We encounter it multiple times. In the story of Noah and the Great Flood, the number seven appears seven times (Gen 5-8). The Israelite tabernacle contained a seven-branched candlestick. In John's Revelation there are seven churches, seven spirits, seven stars, seven seals, and so on. 'Seven' also had cosmic significance for other ancient religions and civilizations.[9]

Historians trace origin of the week all the way back to ancient Babylonia, now part of modern Iraq.[10] This will not surprise anyone who follows the Genesis story of how the Ark of Noah came to rest in the mountainous region of Ararat in far-eastern Turkey (Gen 8:4). From there, Noah and his family would logically have made their way southward into the valleys of the Tigris and Euphrates Rivers, arriving at the "Plain of Shinar" in ancient Babylonia (Gen 11:1,2). If Noah and his family observed the seventh day, which is a fair assumption, the weekly cycle would have been important for them.

The week continues to have global acceptance, in spite of attempts by some governments to shorten or lengthen it. The French Republic implemented a ten-day week in 1793 but abandoned it nine years later. In 1929 the USSR tried a five-day week, and a six-day week in 1931. Social disorder and labor chaos resulted from these attempts to reconfigure the week as God gifted it to humanity at creation.

---

9   The Rig Vega, classical Sanskrit's most holy book of Hinduism and Buddhism, describes seven stars, seven concentric continents, and seven streams. Seven worlds constituted the Indian universe. The Egyptians mapped seven paths to heaven. Islam's Allah created heaven and earth in seven layers, and Buddha at birth took seven strides. See "The Mystical Number 7" (http://www.humanreligions.info/seven.html)

10 "Week" : entry in Wikipedia. (https://en.wikipedia.org/wiki/Week)

A Temple in Time

In our English Bible, the word "Sabbath" makes its first appearance in the sixteenth chapter of Exodus, shortly after the Israelites left Egypt and before they arrived at Mount Sinai. Must we conclude that Sabbath was not observed between creation and the Exodus of Israel from Egypt?[6] The earliest Bible stories are exceedingly brief, but include comments about a few men who followed God in obedience and worship. Enoch obeyed God so perfectly that he was taken to heaven (Gen 5:24). Noah "was a righteous man, blameless among the people of his time, and he walked faithfully with God" (Gen 6:9 TNIV). Abraham "listened to me and obeyed all my requirements, commands, decrees, and instructions" (Gen 26:5 TNIV). Job, living in the patriarchal age and commended by God as blameless, strongly affirmed creation (Job 1:8; 12:7-10). Two Old Testament scholars have found interesting clues about significance of the seventh day in the Hebrew language.[11]

The first thing God made holy was a day of twenty-four hours. He could easily have designated something in space as holy—a sacred mountain perhaps, or a special pond of water—and humans could blow up the mountain or bottle and sell holy water. But God chose a period of time—a day—because only time is beyond human control.

---

11 Samuele Bacchiocchi observes the Hebrew structure of three sentences in Genesis 2:2,3: "On the *seventh day* God ended his work which He had done" (seven Hebrew words).
"He rested on the *seventh day* from all His work which He had done" (seven Hebrew words).
"God blessed the *seventh day* and sanctified it" (seven Hebrew words).
Each sentence in Hebrew contains exactly seven words and the middle word of each sentence is *hassebii*, "seventh day". (Samuele Bacchiocchi, *Divine Rest for Human Restlessness*. Berrien Springs, MI: Biblical Perspectives, 1988), 62,63). Another scholar, Richard Davidson, shows how the Hebrew structure of Psalm 92—composed as "a song for the Sabbath day"—highlights the number seven in fascinating ways. (Richard Davidson, "God's Sabbath Stamp." *Adventist Review*, 195:12, Dec. 2018).

William Johnsson writes: "Today the earth is marred—we have fouled the waters, polluted the atmosphere, and raped the environment. While nature still has power to take our breath away, it is a far cry from its pristine state. But God's temple in time remains unspoiled. It lies beyond the reach of our dirty fingers, inviolate. We can neglect it, refuse it, abandon it, or reject it, but we cannot mar it."[12]

My Takeaway: *God instituted the Seventh Day as the memorial of his creation.*

Your Takeaway?

---

12 William Johnsson, "Gracious Gift of a Living God." *Adventist Review*, August 29, 1996, 12.

A DAY FOR REST

Even youths grow tired and weary,
and young men stumble and fall;
but those who hope in the Lord
will renew their strength.
They will soar on wings like eagles;
they will run and not grow weary,
they will walk and not be faint.
(Isaiah 40:30-31 TNIV)

Time to Rest

Sabbath is first introduced in Scripture as a day for rest. It makes its first biblical appearance in the sixteenth chapter of Exodus, soon after the Israelites crossed the Red Sea. Let us take up the story from there.

The Children of Israel, just released from slavery in Egypt, are slowly making their way through dry lands on the eastern side of the Red Sea. For long-time city-slum dwellers, the journey brings a multitude of strange and scary experiences, but God is using these experiences to teach important lessons. At Marah, where the thirsty travelers encounter pools of bitter water, God sweetens the supply before he also gives this promise: "If you will listen carefully to the voice of the Lord your God and do what is right in his sight, . . . then I will not make you suffer any of the diseases I sent on the Egyptians, for I am the Lord who heals you" (Exod 15:26 NLT). Soon the travelers will be given a lot of instruction about keeping healthy.

As the Israelites continue their desert pilgrimage, sources of food become scarce. God relieves their hunger by providing bread from heaven. The "manna" appears on the ground by sunrise each morning. The people discover a double supply on the sixth day of the week, and Moses explains, "This is what the Lord commanded: Tomorrow is to be a day of sabbath rest, a holy sabbath to the Lord" (Exod 16:23 TNIV). God provides a double portion of manna on Friday and it remains fresh for Sabbath.

Thus God introduced his holy Sabbath to an unruly band of ex-slaves. Forced labor in Egypt—having to find straw to make a daily quota of bricks—did not provide a day of rest. You had to work if you wanted to eat. Incessant toil under the threat of a whipping gave no distinction between one day and another, so Sabbath came to those tired people as a sweet surprise—a weekly gift of rest for weary bodies, rest from a toilsome journey, rest from concerns about daily sustenance. It came as a new experience, a day to enjoy physical rest from work and travel. The one who rescued them from slavery also cared about their physical needs.

SERVANTS AND ANIMALS TOO

The need for rest from physical toil is important, but God had much more to teach the Israelites. He waited until they were safely and comfortably camped near the base of Mount Sinai before introducing himself to them in new ways. They needed to learn that God operates his vast universe and everything in it according to a finely tuned set of laws. At Sinai, he showed them that health and happiness depended on following moral and physical laws. He selected ten statements as moral guidelines; we know them as his Ten Commandments. The Israelites knew instinctively that commands required obedience.

The fourth of those commands related precisely to the weekly day of rest; and the Israelites discovered they were not the only ones to enjoy Sabbath rest. "On that day no one in your household may do any work. That includes you, your sons and daughters, *your male and female servants, your livestock, and any foreigners living among you*" (Exod 20:10 NLT). Those words may have startled the Israelites. Experience had taught them that servants never had a rest day. But God was teaching them that every human being is equal in God's value system. His package includes women, servants, immigrants, refugees, people of every color and conviction.

Sabbath is the day each week when everyone is equal. The boss has no authority over his employees on Sabbath; the employee enjoys Sabbath as a day of freedom from assigned tasks or duties. Sabbath reminds that we are equally created and redeemed by the God of the universe.

This concept was so important that God had to repeat it, sometimes in different ways or with a new emphasis. "Six days do your work" he said, "but on the seventh day do not work, so that your ox and your donkey may rest, and the slave born in your household, and the foreigner among you as well, may be refreshed" (Exod 23:12 TNIV). The idea of a rest-day for work animals must have come as another surprise, but God has a quite different view of his animal creation. Having created every living thing, he respects the need of every creature for periods of physical rest and life enjoyment. In fact, "those who need rest the most—the slave, the resident alien, and the beast of burden—are singled out for special mention. In the rest of the seventh day the underprivileged, even mute animals, find an ally." [13] As we shall see later, God's care extends to the very land itself.

REST AND RELATIONSHIP

After six days of creating, God rested. Was he weary? No. "He will never grow faint or weary" (Isa 40:28 TNIV). I suspect he had two things in mind for day seven. By resting, he was implementing a model for humanity—six days of work followed by a day of rest; and by declaring the day holy, he was making a weekly time for a personal relationship with his human family.

The gift of Sabbath rest supersedes our work and livelihood. "You have six days each week for your ordinary work, but on the seventh day you must stop working, even during the seasons of plowing and harvest" (Exod 34:21 NLT). For that day each week, we forget productivity and profit, grasping and greed. We don't plant or prune. We may forgo a better job or a higher income in order to embrace the blessings of Sabbath. Samuele Bacchiocchi suggests that our work of the six days finds its goal and meaning in the rest of the seventh day. "Resting on the Sabbath means to recognize the meaning of work and of life itself. It means to reject a

---

13   Sigve Tonstad, *The Lost Meaning of the Seventh Day*. [Berrien Springs, MI: Andrews University Press, 2009), 126, 127

lifestyle in which, to achieve comforts and status, one has to submit himself to the idol called work. It means to recognize that work is not a supreme value. It means to acknowledge that God has a claim on all our doing. To accept his claim, we take time out on the Sabbath to praise not the work of our hands but God's working in, for and through our lives." [14]

SOUL REST TOO

During the 1830s the United States government forcibly relocated some native peoples from the crowded east to new Indian Territories in the southwest. Some Cherokee people remembered that journey as "The Trail of Tears." One story tells of an army colonel who was harsh in his administration of the march, forcing mothers with nursing infants to walk many miles every day. Finally, the Cherokee chief called his people to a halt and pleaded passionately, "You must let us stop. Our souls need to catch up with our bodies."[15]

When God created our first parents, he made whole people: "Then the Lord formed a man from the dust of the ground and breathed into his nostrils the breath of life, and the man became *a living being*" (Gen 2:7 TNIV). We are more than bodies.

Twenty-first century lives are crowded with work times, appointments, travel, spending, digital devices, and play. Our need for respite from toil and weariness has reached a critical level in our society. We are stressed out, physically and mentally exhausted, gasping for time to recuperate. One writer observes, "In our stressed-out world in which families are increasingly falling apart and thousands visit hospital emergency rooms each day because their stress has become a major health crisis, we desperately need

---

14 Samuele Bacchiocchi, *Divine Rest for Human Restlessness*. (Berrien Springs, MI: Biblical Perspectives, 1988), 177.
15 Stephen W. Smith, *Soul Custody*. (Colorado Springs, CO: David C. Cook, 2010), 110.

the kind of rest that God offers."[16] He paraphrases Jesus' invitation in Matthew 11:28 this way: "Come unto Me all you who labor to exhaustion, and I will give you rest."

Sabbath is designed to bring restoration to our total being. Writes one believer, "One of my favorite doctrines is the Sabbath. I get stressed out, I get lonely, and I'm disposed to negative thoughts just like everyone else, but for an entire day once a week, I focus on God, rest, family, and friends."[17]

Gerald Schroeder acclaims Sabbath as "the Bible's gift to all humanity, the crown of six days of creation. It is the undersold super-product of the Bible. The essence of the Sabbath is rest."[18] Bacchiocchi adds: "Resting on the Sabbath symbolizes a total response to God, an acceptance of His claim over our work and leisure and an offering to Him of our total being and doing."[19]

"The first Sabbath was celebrated by God to mark the completion of this divine work. This set in motion a pattern for all human beings and for all of life, a sequence of work and rest, from that time on and forever. . . . Only later, following the coming of sin and the consequent degradation of life, does the Sabbath require enforcement."[20]

My Takeaway: *Sabbath is a day of rest after six days of work and stress.*

Your Takeaway?

---

16 Des Cummings, *CREATION Health Discovery*. (Altamonte Springs, FL: CREATION Life, 2016), 32.
17 Adam Fenner, "Is Adventism Relevant Anymore?" *NAD Newspoints*, April 25, 2019.
18 Gerald Schroeder, *The Hidden Face of God*. (New York: Simon and Schuster, 2001), 181.
19 Bacchiocchi, 178.
20 Niels-Erik Andreasen, "A Sabbath Rest for the Whole Earth." *Adventist Review*, August 29, 1996, 21.

4

REST IN ANOTHER DIMENSION

By establishing Sabbath after six days of creating the earth and people, God implemented a cycle of work and rest for all time. In the fourth commandment, "six days you shall labor and do all your work" comes before "the Sabbath of the Lord your God" (Exod 20:9). One writer observes how "experience teaches us that work and rest are two genuine and significant human needs. A person who is workless is one who feels worthless. Work is needed to experience self-worth." [21]

The weary Israelites, traversing the sun-scorched desert on their way to Sinai, were grateful to be given a weekly day of rest. But they were to learn that Sabbath meant more than rest for tired bodies. As we explore the Old Testament, we find some Hebrew words with connotations for our English word "rest", but they do not always carry the same meaning. Two of them are significant in helping us understand the deeper meaning of Sabbath rest.

❖ *Sabat* or *Shabbat*, from which we have the word "Sabbath", means to cease from physical activity. It is the word used in Genesis 2:3 when it says that God rested (*sabat*) from all his work of creation. It is the word Moses used in Exodus 16, when God gave the Israelites the gift of Sabbath rest from labor and travel weariness. It is also the meaning of rest in dozens of Bible passages. Here is a typical reference: "There are six days when you may work, but the seventh is a day of sabbath

---

21 Samuele Bacchiocchi, *Divine Rest for Human Restlessness*. (Berrien Springs, MI: Biblical Perspectives, 1988), 91.

rest [*shabbat*], a day of sacred assembly. You are not to do any work" (Lev 23:3 TNIV).

Everyone needs that kind of rest from hard work, strenuous exercise, and stress. The benefits of the weekly Sabbath include a healthier body, less stress, and increased productivity. Sadly, our society undervalues rest, sometimes equating it with laziness. We praise those who work long hours, seeking to accomplish more and earn more. In short, we are sleep-deprived and rest-less.

❖ There is another Hebrew word for rest: *nuach* (verb) and its related noun, *menuchah*, convey something more than physical rest from labor. These words for "rest" mean to experience stability, security, rest from enemies and trouble, peaceful existence, a state of equilibrium—everything the way it ought to be. It means calm, peace, and tranquility.

Looking ahead to their entry into the Promised Land, God promised the Israelites that they would experience this special and peaceful "rest" from all their wilderness wanderings and hardships. "You will cross the Jordan and settle in the land the Lord your God is giving you as an inheritance, and he will give you rest [*menuchah*] from all your enemies around you so that you will dwell in safety" (Deut 12:10 TNIV). God was promising something they could anticipate with pleasure.

I'm especially noticing the use of *nuach* in the wording of God's fourth commandment: "For in six days the Lord made the heavens and the earth, the sea, and all that is in them, but he rested [*nuach*] on the seventh day. Therefore the Lord blessed the Sabbath day and made it holy" (Exod 20:11 TNIV). This use of *nuach* tells me that after six days of creating, God did not rest because he was tired; he rested in the deeper sense of celebrating the completion of creation. It was a finished work, perfect in every sense. God exhibited no anxiety about the life-giving capacity of his creation. "God knows the world will hold, the plants will perform, and the birds and the fish and the beasts of the field will prosper. All will be well!"[22]

Sabbath was designed to bring that quality of restful experience for us too. It is intended to be more than a once-weekly rest from hard work and effort. It comes as a gift of grace, bringing peace and stability, a sense of contentment when we hand over control to the one who creates, sustains, and provides security and peace of mind from the troubles and disappointments that plague our restless lives. In the following piece, Uche Ikpa is writing about the promise of Sabbath rest in the Book of Hebrews (Heb 4).

"What does God's rest signify spiritually? The rest talked about here is deep and profound. It is that which sums up the end game of our existence on earth, and how we can live in peace and rest, despite being poor or rich. It is peaceful existence that enhances and enriches your life here on earth, and when over on earth, continues in the hereafter. This is a promise God has given to humanity. The Scripture reminds us that it is about obedience to God's word. Those who heard it in the wilderness perished because they did not believe the word of God. . . . Many are still perishing today because they will not accept God's word that will save and heal them."[23]

Jack Dawson is a Christian artist whose canvas reproductions are collected and loved by thousands. One of his paintings, "Peace in the Midst of the Storm", depicts a small bird sheltering on its nest in a tiny rock crevice while a frightening storm lashes the cliff face. That is the kind of peace that Sabbath is intended to bring you and me. But it does not come easily in our storm-ravished world. It is hard to enjoy that Sabbath peace and tranquility when we are trying to cope with a difficult financial issue, a terminal illness, a threatening divorce, or fear from any cause. That is when we must learn to trust our heavenly Father, casting all our cares upon Him (Psalm 55:22; 1 Peter 5:7).

---

22 Walter Brueggemann, *Sabbath as Resistance: Saying No to the Culture of Now.* (Louisville, KY: Westminster John Knox Press, 2017), 29.
23 Uche Ikpa, "Encouraged Strongly to Enter into God's Rest." Cambridge Community Television. (https://www.cctvcambridge.org/node/127874)

Jack Dawson's painting illustrates the kind of peace that characterizes true Sabbath rest—a freedom from the grinding stress and agitation of twenty-first century life on this planet. It is also the quality of rest Jesus was talking about when he shared his invitation: "Come to me, all you who are weary and burdened, and I will give you rest" (Matt 11:28 TNIV).[24] Here, the Greek words for "rest" is *anapausis*, the closest equivalent to the Hebrew *menuchah*. Matthew follows this invitation with the Sabbath story of the walk through the grain fields and Jesus' announcement that he is Lord of the Sabbath, the day for soul rest (Matt 12:1-8).

We observe that quality of peaceful rest in the life of Jesus. While his disciples battled a windstorm on Galilee, their master slept peacefully at the back of the boat (Mark 4:37,38). Several times during his ministry, Jesus took a winding path from Jerusalem over the Mount of Olives to Bethany, his favorite village. His destination was the home of Martha, Mary, and Lazarus, two sisters and a brother who were always ready to welcome the itinerant Christ and minister lovingly to his needs for rest and sustenance. There was something important about those visits to Bethany. No one in the history of the universe has ever carried an agenda as momentous as our Lord. His life here on earth was so brief, his ministry so crammed into three short years, his priorities so crucial for our salvation. Yet he took time out to rest, secure and at peace in the care of his Father.

It is beautiful to think of Sabbath as an island of tranquility surrounded by the restless sea and rough weather that characterizes the days of our week. That peace, that quality of *menuchah* should impact our outlook and behavior through the entire week. Allow the peace and serenity of Sabbath to overflow into the workdays that follow. John Walton writes:

"When we 'rest' on the sabbath, we recognize [God] as the author of order and the one who brings rest (stability) to our lives and world. We take our hands off the controls of our lives and

---

24 Here the Greek word for "rest" is *anapausis*, the closest equivalent of the Hebrew *menuchah*.

acknowledge him as the one who is in control. Most importantly, this calls on us to step back from our workaday world—those means by which we try to provide for ourselves and gain control of our circumstances. Sabbath is for recognizing that it is God who provides for us and who is master of our lives and our world."[25]

Walter Brueggemann, remembering an old catch-line for Coca Cola, says succinctly, "Sabbath is not simply 'the pause that refreshes.' It is the pause that transforms."[26]

Beyond the present, there will be a day when the crises of life are finally past; then we will experience fully the Sabbath peace. "There remains, then, a Sabbath-rest for the people of God" (Heb 4:9 TNIV).[27] "Sabbath rest is not merely a means to recover lost energies, but primarily a means to experience in this restless age the divine rest and peace of salvation already available as well as a foretaste of the greater rest and joy awaiting God's people in the kingdom of glory."[28]

My Takeaway: *Sabbath impacts my outlook and behavior through the entire week.*

Your Takeaway ?

---

[25] John H. Walton, *The Lost World of Genesis One.* (Downers Grove IL: IVP Academic, 2009), 147.

[26] Brueggemann, 45.

[27] For a discussion of the meaning of Sabbath "rest" in Hebrews 4:9, see Skip MacCarty, *In Granite or Ingrained? What the Old and New Covenants reveal about the Gospel, the Law, and the Sabbath.* (Berrien Springs, MI: Andrews Univ. Press, 2007), 227.

[28] Bacchiocchi, 178

5

REST FOR THE OPPRESSED

We have talked about our need for physical and peaceful rest, but there is another kind of "rest" that is desperately needed in our world. We are talking about the heartbreaking circumstances of an estimated 25 million refugees; the 40 million men, women, and children enslaved in forced labor, human trafficking, sexual exploitation, and forced marriages.[29] We must add blatant racism and domestic abuse. These devastating realities characterize our contemporary world. Sadly, the cry of the oppressed is too often muffled by the roar and racket of our surroundings.

God's concern for the poor comes through powerfully in the Bible. Through Moses, God introduced laws of social justice for the poor in Israel. "At the end of every seventh year [the sabbath year or sabbatical] you must cancel the debts of everyone who owes you money" (Deut 15:1 NLT). And every forty-ninth year—designated as a Year of Jubilee—"each of you may return to the land that belonged to your ancestors" (Lev 25:10-13 NLT).[30] If you were forced to sell your ancestral land because of poverty, you were to get it back. If poverty forced you into virtual slavery for survival, you regained your personal freedom at the Jubilee (Lev 25:23-55). We may smile at these ancient practices that are foreign to our economy, but in the biblical view, creditors and the wealthy shared some of the responsibility for poverty and indebtedness. When Jesus taught his

---

29 Statistics for 1919 are from the United Nations Refugee Agency and the International Labor Organization.
30 Based on the reading of Leviticus 25, some argue that the Jubilee was every 50th year; however, most Jewish scholars confirm a 49-year cycle for the Jubilee (see "Jubilee [biblical]" in *Wikipedia*).

disciples to pray, "Forgive us our debts, as we also have forgiven our debtors" (Matt 6:12 TNIV), he doubtless had more than sins in mind. The Sabbath commandment addresses the equality of all people. "The seventh day is a Sabbath to the Lord your God. On it you shall not do any work, neither you, nor your son or daughter, nor your male or female *servant* (read "*slave*"), nor your animals, nor any *foreigner* (read "*refugee*") residing in your towns" (Exod 20:11 TNIV). Sabbath calls for equality between male and female, slave and free, alien and citizen. Every person—race, color, or creed—is equal in God's value system. "The Sabbath changes the tyranny of injustice and announces in real time that no one is to be left behind in the rut of powerlessness."[31]

So, the Lord's instructions to Israel were clear: "True justice must be given to foreigners living among you and to orphans. When you are harvesting your crops and forget to bring in a bundle of grain from your field, don't go back to get it. Leave it for the foreigners, orphans, and widows. Then the Lord will bless you in all you do. Always remember that you were slaves in Egypt and that the Lord your God redeemed you from your slavery" (Deut 24:17-19 NLT).

God's hatred of social injustice comes through in these words shouted to the people of Israel by Amos: "Listen to this, you who rob the poor and trample down the needy! You can't wait for the Sabbath day to be over so you can get back to cheating the helpless. You measure out grain with dishonest measures and cheat the buyer with dishonest scales. And you mix the grain you sell with chaff swept from the floor. Then you enslave poor people for one silver coin or a pair of sandals" (Amos 8:4-6 NLT). The prophet had more: "I hate all your show and pretense—the hypocrisy of your religious festivals and solemn assemblies. Away with your noisy hymns of praise! Instead, I want to see a mighty flood of justice" (Amos 5:21-24 NLT).

Sadly, Israel failed to make the connection between their Sabbath worship and their responsibility to the needy. They were

---

31 Dan Allender, *Sabbath*. (Nashville, TN: Thomas Nelson, 2009), 179.

A Day for Joy

fastidious in formal worship, prayers, and fasting, and expressed surprise when God was not pleased. "We have fasted before you," they said. "Why aren't you impressed?" God responded: "This is the kind of fasting I want: free those who are wrongly imprisoned; lighten the burden of those who work for you. Share your food with the hungry, and give shelter to the homeless. Give clothes to those who need them, and do not hide from relatives who need your help." God connected those instructions to their Sabbath-keeping: "Keep the Sabbath day holy. *Don't pursue your own interests* on that day. Honor the Sabbath in everything you do on that day, and *don't follow your own desires* or talk idly. Then the Lord will be your delight" (Isa 58:3,6,7,13,14 NLT).

JESUS THE LIBERATOR

On a Sabbath day in Nazareth, a young teacher, recently baptized in the Jordan by John the Baptist, was worshipping at the synagogue with the villagers, as he had always done (Luke 4:16). Everyone in the congregation knew this young man. Jesus was a "local boy". He belonged to the family of Mary and Joseph, known and respected residents of Nazareth.

Given an opportunity to address the congregation, Jesus opened the scroll of the prophet Isaiah and read, "The Spirit of the Lord is upon me, because he has anointed me to preach the gospel to the poor; he has sent me to heal the brokenhearted, to proclaim liberty to the captives, and recovery of sight to the blind, to set at liberty those who are oppressed; to proclaim the acceptable year of the Lord" (Luke 4:18,19 NKJV, Isa 61:1,2). Rolling up the scroll, he handed it to the attendant, sat down, looked directly at the congregation, and said, "Today this Scripture is fulfilled in your hearing" (Luke 4:20,21 NKJV).

Those words of Jesus were pregnant with meaning. As God in the flesh, he was here as a liberator with a mission to "set free." His ministry would bring good news to the poor, release from all kinds of suffering, and salvation from sin. During his three-and-a-half-year ministry, Jesus fulfilled that mission of justice for the oppressed and downtrodden. "A bruised reed he will not break, and a dimly burning wick he will not quench; he will faithfully bring forth justice" (Isa 42:3 NRSV). The four gospels are loaded with stories of people healed of their diseases, freed from demon possession, and given hope and wholeness.

My Brother's Keeper

When God confronted Cain about his sin, the young man shrugged and responded, "Am I my brother's keeper (Gen 4:9 TNIV)?" The question still hangs, unanswered and ignored by millions who populate our planet. And it's hard to answer the question when your mailbox is cluttered with appeals from innumerable charities; when the day's news features the plight of desperate refugees turned away by fear; when families in Sudan are perishing with hunger; when children in Kenya are dying because their only source of water is polluted; when you encounter a homeless person on the street.

Yes, it's hard to be the answer to Cain's question. It was hard for a Samaritan trekking the lonely and dangerous road to Jericho when he encountered a wounded victim of terrorism—a Jew—on the roadside. In a different scenario, the victim might have spat in his direction. Today the traveler saw a "brother" in desperate need.

I was not there on the road to Jericho. There are no refugees on my doorstep. Sudan and Kenya seem like places on another planet. I'll miss my dental appointment if I stop to help this person on the street. And I can't donate to *all* those charities.

But I *can* do something. Christ is asking me, someone he redeemed on Calvary, to answer Cain's question. He will help open my eyes and bring into focus some needs in my community. I can allocate time to sit at someone's bedside. I can open my purse wider in response to pleas from ADRA and other organizations working on the ground. And I can pray a lot more, because my God cares and responds when he reads my heart. I remember how he cared deeply about an abused and abandoned slave woman in the wilderness of Beersheba (Gen 21:8-20.)

Jesus emphasized our responsibility to the poor and needy. He said the final judgment will not be about what we believe or how often we worship, but how we have lived. "Then the King will say to those on his right, 'Come, you who are blessed by my Father. Take your inheritance. . . I was hungry and you gave me something to eat, I was thirsty and you gave me something to drink, I was a stranger and you invited me in, I needed clothes and you clothed me, I was sick and you looked after me, I was in prison and you came to visit me. . . Whatever you did for one of the least of these brothers and sisters of mine, you did for me'" (Matt 25:34-40 TNIV).

Our Sabbath worship is meaningless, even offensive, when we ignore the social and economic needs of the human community. But when we practice God's love his way, we are ready, in Kendra Haloviak Valentine's words, to sing the Sabbath song. "It is a song by people who once were slaves, but who are now free. A song of hope envisioning an alternative future that begins today. It is a song anticipating a new earth, where injustice is removed forever by the very presence of God. When we keep the Sabbath, we sing God's song." [32]

My Takeaway: *Sabbath calls me to care for people in desperate need.*

Your Takeaway?

---

32 Kendra Haloviak, "The Sabbath Song." *Adventist Review*, August 29, 1996, 35.

A DAY FOR RELATIONSHIP

Look!
I stand at the door and knock.
If you hear my voice
and open the door,
I will come in,
and we will share a meal together
as friends.
(Revelation 3:20 NLT)

HAND MADE

One of the compelling insights from the story of Jesus is the picture he paints of God. In a society that marginalized women, tax collectors, the poor, the widows, the sick and the blind, Jesus spent a lot of his time bonding with these people: eating with sinners, healing the sick, making friends with the lonely. If Jesus placed such value on relationships when he was on earth, shouldn't we expect to find this exemplified when he created people?

We are not disappointed. The Genesis account is a beautiful description of how God made people, in contrast to the way he simply *spoke* most other things into existence. "By the word of the Lord the heavens were made," wrote the psalmist. "For he *spoke* and it came to be; he *commanded*, and it stood firm" (Psalm 33:6,9 TNIV). Notice these examples:

- "And God said, 'Let there be light,' and there was light" (Gen 1:3 TNIV).
- "Then God said, 'Let the land produce vegetation.' And it was so" (1:11).
- And God said, 'Let the land produce living creatures according to their kinds.' And it was so" (1:24)

Suddenly, though, we encounter a change in God's mode of creating. On day six God said, "Let us *make* human beings in our image, in our likeness, so that they may rule over the fish in the sea and the birds in the sky, over the livestock and all the wild animals, and over all the creatures that move along the ground." The story confirms that God carried out his plan. "He *created* human beings in his own image. . . . male and female he created them" (Gen 1:26,27 TNIV).[33]

The second chapter of Genesis describes *how* he did it: "Then the Lord formed a man from the dust of the ground, and breathed into his nostrils the breath of life, and the man became *a living being*" (Gen 2:7 TNIV). God created the human as *a wholistic being*, a oneness of body, mind, and spirit. The Hebrew word *nephesh*, translated as "soul" in the King James Bible, has the meaning of a "living being", as in the newer translations.

Genesis goes on to tell how Eve was made. "The Lord caused the man to fall into a deep sleep, and while he was sleeping, he took one of the man's ribs and then closed up the place with flesh. Then the Lord made a woman from the rib he had taken out of the man" (Gen 2:22 TNIV). The Genesis story is familiar to us, but let's make it come alive with a little imagination.[34]

> So we find God busy doing something here in a forest glade. Down on hands and knees, he takes golden soil and works it with his fingers. The universe watches, spellbound, as he forms a completely new creature, a human. When the task is completed, he bends down, kisses the lips, breathes into the nostrils, and watches as the eyes open. Then, smiling, he draws the man to his feet, a tall, majestic figure, his bronze body a match for the ochre brown of the soil. "I want you to meet Adam," God says, and it seems the whole universe erupts with shouts of joy.[35]

> But God is not finished. "Watch now." The onlookers anticipate he will take more soil and form a second human, but God has a different plan. Bidding Adam lie down in the soft grass, he allows him to sleep. While the man dreams of

---

33 We should not read "in his image" to mean a physical likeness to God, who is "spirit".
34 Adapted from the author's "On the Sixth Day", published in a blog, November 5, 2015 by *Adventist Today*.
35 The Book of Job describes heavenly beings present at the creation (Job 38:4-7).

happiness, God gently removes a small rib from his chest, close to his heart. With deft fingers, he manipulates the small bone and within minutes has formed the body of a beautiful woman. Looking on with admiration, the entire universe breaks into galaxies of praise: "the morning stars sang together, and all the angels shouted for joy" (Job 38:7 TNIV). They have witnessed the crowning acts of creation. And even as they sing, the liquid notes of God's voice are heard. "My work of creation is complete. It is all very good."

From the Genesis account of beginnings, we learn something important about ourselves as human beings. Our existence is not accidental. We did not evolve. We are God's workmanship—hand made. In spectacular fashion, God *spoke* the world and everything in it into existence, but with his own hands he lovingly formed the bodies of Adam and Eve. Then, having spent six days building a magnificent home for his human creatures, God took time on day seven to walk and talk with them, enjoying an intimate and beautiful togetherness. He took time to bond with them (Gen 3:8,9). We call that "relationship."

God gave so much of Himself when he made humanity. He endowed them with unique qualities which were not conferred on the animal creation. By making humans "in his image", God shared some of his divine attributes with them. With the gift of a mind he endowed humans with a capacity to comprehend, know, analyze, decide, and be conscious of their own existence. With the gift of free choice, he gave the ability to experience his love and to exhibit that love in their relationships with each other. With the gift of management, he gave them authority over the earth he had made for them. And with the gift of Sabbath, God gave his human creatures a time to remember who they were and to celebrate their special relationship to him.

A DAY FOR RELATIONSHIP

As the Israelites, so recently released from Egyptian bondage, adapted to a nomadic lifestyle, God surprised them with the gift of a weekly rest day, something that their generation had not experienced. When they arrived at a wide plain near Mount Sinai, Moses directed them into an organized encampment for an extended period of instruction. Part of the instruction included giving Ten Rules as guides for their living. The fourth of those Rules gave them a new and important reason for their Sabbath keeping—it celebrated their relationship with God, because of his unique and beautiful act of creation (Exod 20:11).

Although sin marred the original, unblemished relationship with God and each other by introducing guilt, fear, and shame, God continually sought ways to renew the friendship. On the plain at Sinai, he demonstrated his desire to do that by adding his own special tent to the Hebrew encampment. Each Sabbath came as a special time to worship the Creator God who made and loved them. Worship will always be the appropriate response to that knowledge.

We must think of relationship as a two-way street. Relationship with the Creator God requires our participation. We must immerse ourselves in the Scriptures where the God of the universe talks to us and shows us the extent of his love and grace. We respond by talking to him during quiet moments of prayer, sharing our inner feelings and needs. Reading God's Word in dialogue with him lies at the heart of a living and learning relationship.

The Christian believer enjoys two levels of relationship—upward and outward. God gave us Sabbath to connect at the highest level—a time when creator and creature share fellowship time together. Relationship on a horizontal level is also what Sabbath is about. We were created for togetherness. One of the sad realities of our technological world is the loss of intimacy. People are lonely, craving affection. We are desperate for relationship.

Someone has said, "If we don't know *who* we are, we will not know *why* we are." [36] Was that thought running through David's mind when he wrote, "When I look at the night sky and see the work of your fingers—the moon and the stars you set in place—

---

[36] David Asscherick is credited with the statement at the opening of a Global Youth Leaders Congress in Kassel, Germany, in 2018.

what are mere mortals that you should think about them, human beings that you should care for them? Yet you made them only a little lower than God and crowned them with glory and honor. You gave them charge over everything you made, putting all things under their authority" (Psalm 8:3-6 NLT). Sabbath reminds us *why* we are here. "God could have finished his act of creation without making a Sabbath, but he established it so he could fellowship with man in a special way. He wanted to be not only our creator but also our Friend. . . . The Sabbath is God's gift to us of himself." [37]

There is a powerful relationship between the human creation and Sabbath. When we detach Sabbath from creation, we disregard God's holy purpose in placing it there as a symbol of his relationship with us. Sigve Tonstad compares the seventh day to a nation's flag: "We should resist the eclipse of the seventh day as much as we are likely to resist the replacement of the flag of the nation we love and cherish." [38]

My Takeaway: *Sabbath tells me who I am and why I'm here.*

Your Takeaway?

---

[37] Sakae Kubo, *God Meets Man: A Theology of the Sabbath and the Second Advent.* (Nashville, TN: Southern Publishing Association, 1978), 16,17.

[38] Sigve Tonstad, *The Lost Meaning of the Seventh Day.* (Berrien Springs, MI: Andrews University Press, 2009), 9.

7

Designed by God

The Sabbath commandment tells why we are here. It is because the God of the universe is our maker and friend. We stand in awe of his creation, the breathtaking beauty of it all, the miracle of life. But sometimes we overlook the miracle of ourselves. The human body, with its complexity and functions, was *designed* by the Creator God. Your body carries God's signature. It is like an invisible trademark: "*Designed by God.*" Think about that!

Despite the compounding effects of sin and degradation, the human body is unique and sacred. That remains true even when your body is ravished by sickness; it may be missing a limb or two because of accident or disease; it may have lost its capacity to think and remember; it may be a pitiful reflection of the "image" that God set in place. But whatever its condition, your body establishes your identity as God's human creation. It carries the creator's signature. For that reason, it must be nourished, cared for, respected, and never abused. "You do not belong to yourself," Paul reminded his readers, "so you must honor God with your body" (1 Cor 6:20 NLT).

In poetic form, King David expressed amazement about God's intimate knowledge of him, including the wonder and workings of his own body. Listen:

> "O Lord, you have examined my heart
> and know everything about me.
> You know when I sit down or stand up.
> You know my thoughts even when I'm far away.
> You see me when I travel and when I rest at home.

> You know everything I do. . . .
> You made all the delicate, inner parts of my body
> and knit me together in my mother's womb.
> Thank you for making me so wonderfully complex!
> Your workmanship is marvelous—how well I know it.
> You watched me as I was being formed in utter seclusion,
> as I was woven together in the dark of the womb.
> You saw me before I was born.
> Every day of my life was recorded in your book.
> Every moment was laid out before a single day had passed.
> How precious are your thoughts about me, O God.
> They cannot be numbered!
> I can't even count them;
> they outnumber the grains of sand"
> (Psalm 139:1-3,13-18 NLT)!

Since the day when David shared those reflections, science has made incredible discoveries about the human organism. Gerald Schroeder, a respected scientist in the fields of nuclear and molecular physics, expresses his amazement at the complexity of our human bodies: "The human body acts as a finely tuned machine, a magnificent metropolis in which, as its inhabitants, each of the 75 trillion cells, composed of 10^{27} atoms, moves in symbiotic precision. . . . Ten to the twenty-seventh power—a one followed by twenty-seven zeros, a thousand million million million million atoms—are organized by a single act when a protozoan-like sperm cell adds its message of genetic material into a receptive egg cell. Combined, these two miniscule cells contain all the information needed to produce the entire body at each stage of its growth, from fetus to adult. We are so embedded in the biosphere that the marvel of its organization has become lost within its commonness. . . . A single cell at fertilization contained within it all the potential that you were ever physically to become. And every cell within your body retains that wisdom."[39]

---

[39] Gerald Schroeder, *The Hidden Face of God*. (New York: Simon & Schuster, 2001), 49, 87.

A Day for Joy 39

David concluded the contemplation of his body with a prayer: "Search me, O God, and know my heart; test me and know my anxious thoughts. Point out anything in me that offends you and lead me along the path of everlasting life" (Psalm 139:23,24 NLT).

Keeping It Healthy

Given that God designed the human body, he must be deeply interested in our physical and mental health. He responded caringly to Elijah's emotional crisis when the depressed prophet crawled into a cave in the mountain wilderness (1 Kings 19:1-18). Generations later, Jesus performed multiple healings for bodies and minds. Each Sabbath comes as a time for emotional healing.

God gave the ancient Israelites a lot of instruction about caring for their health. If they listened and obeyed his instructions, God would keep his promise of protection from the diseases that ravaged the Egyptians (Exod 15:26). In contrast to the harmful medical practices of the Egyptians, the Mosaic health laws were light years ahead of their time.

Sim McMillen, a medical doctor, made a study of ancient Egyptian medical documents dating from the time of Moses.[40] He found that while ancient Egypt led the world in the knowledge of human anatomy and surgical techniques[41], the story was quite different in the treatment of illness and disease. The Ebers Papyrus,[42] dating to 1550 B.C., the time of Moses, records prescriptions, magical formulas, incantations, and many foul remedies, including the use of animal dung for healing wounds and for contraception. Such practices led to the spread of infection and frequent death.

---

40 S.I. McMillen and David Stern, *None of These Diseases*. Revised ed. (Grand Rapids, MI: Revell, 2000).
41 In 2009 I visited the Kom Ombo Temple in Upper Egypt. Built during the Ptolemaic dynasty (180 – 47 B.C.), one wall contains carvings of dozens of medical and surgical instruments in use at that time. Many are remarkably similar to surgical instruments used today.
42 "Ancient Egyptian Medicine." (Wikipedia).

Leprosy was rarely recognized as a highly infectious disease, so there was little attempt to isolate or quarantine the sufferer.

Moses received his formal education in Egypt, but God later gave him inspired counsel on health that was 3,500 years ahead of its time.[43] The Mosaic health laws focused on the *prevention* of disease, cleansing by *frequent washing*, proper *disposal of waste*, *quarantine* for infectious diseases, and choice of *clean foods*.

Sadly, and incredibly, most of God's health instruction was ignored and lost through subsequent centuries. Some of those basic health rules were not re-discovered until the second half of the nineteenth century. Some of it is still being validated, particularly in the field of nutrition.

Although our bodies are warped and wounded by too many years of sin and suffering, it does not lessen our Father's love for us as his children. Jesus demonstrated that love in his healing ministry with all classes and ages. The Sabbath, dating all the way back to creation, is a weekly reminder that our bodies are God's workmanship, carrying his trademark. "Do you not know," Paul questioned, "that your bodies are temples of the Holy Spirit, who is in you, whom you have received from God" (1 Cor.6:19 TNIV)? The apostle strikes an even higher note when he says, "I urge you, brothers and sisters, in view of God's mercy, to offer your bodies as a living sacrifice, holy and pleasing to God—this is true worship" (Rom 12:1 TNIV). Paul is telling us that keeping a healthy body and mind is one way by which we worship our Creator. There is an integral relationship between the Sabbath, our bodies, and our worship.

Keeping my body healthy means avoiding the things that cause it harm. Paul counseled, "Put to death whatever belongs to your earthly nature: sexual immorality, impurity, lust, evil desires and

---

[43] Some Mosaic practices may reflect commonly accepted cultural beliefs and practices of the time. The test for a wife's infidelity, recorded in Numbers 5:11-31, makes no sense to us today and would be considered an abuse of a woman's rights.

A Day for Joy

greed, which is idolatry" (Col 3:5 TNIV). On the flip side, I should practice excellent habits of daily living.

Our bodies are a long way from God's ideal. King David understood that: "My health may fail, and my spirit may grow weak, but God remains the strength of my heart; he is mine forever" (Psalm 73:26 NLT). To the extent that we are capable, we have a divine obligation to keep our minds and bodies in the best possible condition. Florida-based CREATION Life offers eight recommendations for doing that, based on the eight letters of the word CREATION.[44] All have their origin in the Eden world of our first parents.

CHOICE. At creation, God built freedom into the human mind. Adam and Eve were given the ability to choose and make decisions. So, choice becomes the first step toward improving our health and well-being. "Give careful thought to the paths for your feet and be steadfast in all your ways," Solomon admonishes (Prov 4:26 TNIV).

REST. Rest empowers us to function at our best. God made provision for a weekly rest day by establishing Sabbath. We have talked about our need for rest from toil and anxiety. "It is useless for you to work so hard from early morning until late at night, anxiously working for food to eat; for God gives rest to his loved ones" (Psalm 127:2 NLT).

ENVIRONMENT. God provided the first humans with a perfect environment for life and activity. "God saw all that he had made, and it was very good" (Gen 1:31 TNIV). Sin has destroyed that perfect world. Living today, we must understand how our work and home environments impact our health. We also share responsibility to protect our planet from abuse and needless destruction.

ACTIVITY. In giving humans management of the earth he had created, God provided for rewarding and beneficial activity. Neuroscientists are discovering that physical exercise is a pre-req-

---

44 Altamonte Springs, FL: CREATION Life.

uisite for healthy brain function.[45] Scripture does not have much direct counsel about exercise because people in Bible times walked nearly everywhere they went. Paul knew that an exercise program requires a lot of self-discipline: "I discipline my body and bring it into subjection" (1 Cor 9:27 NKJV).

TRUST. The Edenic relationship was one of perfect trust, vertically and horizontally. Sabbath generates trust as we worship our Creator-Redeemer. Dependence on God relieves anxiety. "Trust in the Lord with all your heart; do not depend on your own understanding" (Prov 3:5 NLT).

INTERPERSONAL RELATIONSHIPS. God said, "It is not good for the man to be alone." We are better together (Gen 2:18). Loneliness in the crowd is a growing problem in many parts of the world. Families that pray and play together stay together. "Dear friends, let us love one another, for love comes from God" (1 John 4:7 TNIV).

OUTLOOK. A positive attitude is important to our well-being. "A cheerful heart is good medicine, but a broken spirit saps a person's strength" (Prov 17:22 NLT). "A peaceful heart leads to a healthy body" (Prov 14:30 NLT).

NUTRITION. God's original diet for humankind was plant-based (Gen 1:29). A whole-food, plant-based diet has been repeatedly shown to help prevent disease, but also to arrest and even reverse it. Paul wrote, "Whether you eat or drink or whatever you do, do it all for the glory of God" (1 Cor 10:31 TNIV).

My Takeaway: *Sabbath challenges me to keep my body and mind clean and healthy*

Your Takeaway?

---

[45] John J. Ratey, *Spark: The Revolutionary New Science of Exercise and the Brain.* (New York: Little, Brown, 2008).

8
The Gifted Earth

Most of us belong to the "indoor generation", which is a major departure from the way life used to be. Over the course of two centuries, workers have migrated from workplaces like fields and farms to factories and offices. "Instead of basking in natural sunlight, many people today are spending the majority of their times basking in the glow of some kind of screen."[46] That pretty much described my vocation as a librarian; except that my love of nature and wide-open sky took me on extended backpacking trips into the Australian wilderness. On warm summer nights, in my sleeping bag, sans tent, I watched the Southern Cross blaze its trajectory across the heavens. My work-a-day world receded and the master of the universe became an awesome reality. I felt at-one with King David, who spent years of his life outdoors and recorded dozens of psalms about a God who became very real to him. "When I look at the night sky and see the work of your fingers, what are mere mortals that you should think about them" (Psalm 8:3,4 NLT)?

After filling the planet with an infinite and breathtaking variety of creatures, God told Adam and Eve about the relationship they would have with his creation: "Rule over the fish in the sea and the birds in the sky and over living creatures that move on the ground" (Gen 1:28 TNIV). To illustrate what he meant, God brought some animals to Adam for him to discover their unique characteristics (Gen 2:19,20).

When God made his covenant with Noah after the great Flood, he said something that may surprise you: "I now establish

---
46 Stephen Walden, *USA Today*, May 2018.

my covenant with you and with your descendants after you *and with every living creature that was with you—the birds, the livestock and all the wild animals, all those that came out of the ark with you—every living creature on earth*" (Gen 9:9,10 TNIV). Amazing! Even rhinos, kangaroos, and baboons were included in that covenant.

We share a commonality with the animal creation. Job clearly understood that all God's creatures receive their life from him, who is their maker and sustainer. Listen: "Ask the beasts, and they will teach you; and the birds of the air, and they will tell you; or speak to the earth, and it will teach you; and the fish of the sea will explain to you. Who among all these does not know that the hand of the Lord has done this, *in whose hand is the life of every living thing, and the breath of all mankind*" (Job 12:7-10 NKJV)?

No surprise then that God seeks relationship with his entire creation. His care and concern for his creation has no limits. Whether spoken into existence or handmade, everything is important to the Creator-God. We saw that Sabbath rest was prescribed for animals in the service of people. Wild creatures enjoy a rhythm of life that provides resting periods. Psalm 104, King David's hymn about creation, shows how everything—the earth, the seasons, the environment—is wonderfully planned and integrated.

When Jonah was angry with God for withholding destruction from Nineveh after the people repented, God responded that he had more than people in mind: "Should I not have concern for the great city of Nineveh, in which there are more than a hundred and twenty thousand people who cannot tell their right hand from their left—*and also many animals*" (Jonah 4:11 TNIV)? As Jesus observed the anxious faces of people who struggled to make ends meet, he challenged them to think about God's care for his wild creatures. "Look at the birds of the air," he said, "your heavenly Father feeds them" (Matt 6:26 TNIV). "Are not two sparrows sold for a penny? Yet not one of them will fall to the ground outside your Father's care" (Matt 10:29 TNIV).

Wisdom in Nature

The wisdom God has given to wild creatures is amazing. Nearly 2,000 species of birds migrate long distances each year. The record is held by the Arctic Tern which flies from Arctic breeding grounds all the way to Antarctica and back every year. Species of butterflies, hummingbirds, fish, and turtles, among other wildlife, follow long seasonal migration routes.

King Solomon studied the wisdom of small creatures. "Four things on earth are small, yet they are extremely wise," he said. "Ants are creatures of little strength, yet they store up their food in the summer; hyraxes are creatures of little power, yet they make their home in the crags; locusts have no king, yet they advance together in ranks." Fourth on his list were gecko lizards which Solomon could catch with his hands, yet they found their way into his palace (Prov 30:24-28 TNIV)!

At the opposite end of the scale is God's description of "behemoth, which I made along with you and which feeds on grass like an ox" (Job 40:15-24 TNIV). Some scholars identify this large and powerful animal with the African Bush Elephant, the world's largest land mammal, weighing in at around 6,500 pounds. Elephants are herbivores, and share several human characteristics. [47]

My appreciation for elephants grew from observations of these highly intelligent, social animals in several parts of Africa, including the Sheldrick Elephant Orphanage near Nairobi, Kenya, named in honor of David and Daphne Sheldrick, who spent most of their lives rescuing and caring for orphaned elephants. Like many other

---

[47] The family bond between elephants is strong. A missing member is welcomed back with much touching and intertwining of trunks. Empathy for an injured young one or adult is demonstrated by touching and communication noises. Mourning for a dead baby is long and often teary. Elephants have been seen to spend time with a bereaved family member, with much touching of trunks. Mischief among teenage elephants replicates typical human teen behavior. (Information from *Africa Geographic*, (https://africageographic.com/blog/17-elephant-facts-you-need-to-know/)

animals, elephants have a mysterious ability to communicate with each other. They also have fantastic memories.

Does God communicate with wild creatures? Orphaned elephants, frequently rescued when poachers kill their mothers, have an in-bread fear of humans, but Daphne tells of a night when her husband was stranded in the wilderness, four hours from home. Two orphaned elephants, transitioning to the wild, found David and guided him home. "What touched him most was that they seemed to understand that he was disadvantaged in the dark and knew that he needed guidance. As it became darker, they pressed closer to him, until he found himself sandwiched between [them], the pace of their walk adjusted to match his own. He knew that they passed other groups of elephants in the dark, as he could hear them and even smell them, and it surprised him that the orphans avoided contact, presumably because they knew that David's presence would be unwelcome." The experience made a deep impression on David. "It was such a humbling and stirring experience. I felt at one with them in their world, entirely dependent on them for my safety, sheltered and protected as if I were one of their own." [48]

Stories like that are evidence that God communicates with wild creatures. He has equipped birds and animals with a degree of trust in him as their creator and sustainer, and we humans are sometimes recipients of that trust.

Earth Management

At creation, God gave humans the task of earth management, but we have largely failed in our stewardship. While Israel was encamped at Mount Sinai, God looked ahead to their arrival in the Promised Land: "When you enter the land I am going to give you, the land itself must observe a sabbath to the Lord. For six years sow your fields, and for six years prune your vineyards and gather their crops. *But in the seventh year the land is to have a year of sabbath rest*" (Lev 25:2,3 TNIV). God would reward faithfulness with an abun-

[48] Daphne Sheldrick, *Love, Life, and Elephants*. (New York: Farrar, Straus, 2012), 113

A Day for Joy

dant harvest every sixth year. Just as every seventh *day* was a rest for people and their animals, every seventh *year* was to be a "sabbath" rest for the land. It was a caring and sensible provision which, if followed, would guard the soil against depletion of nutrients and erosion. The principle of caring for the earth that we occupy and work applies everywhere and always.

God's original plant-based diet for humanity was modified after sin invaded our planet. God's covenant with Noah after the Flood included use of some animals for human sustenance. However, his covenant never included killing of animals for sport and pleasure, nor the slaughtering of elephants and rhinos for their ivory. Other animals are killed for supposed medicinal properties which have never been proven. "The righteous care for the needs of their animals," observed Solomon, "but the kindest acts of the wicked are cruel" (Prov 12:10 TNIV).

In earth's final hour, God says he will destroy those who ravage his creation (Rev 11:19). "Suddenly our Sabbath contemplation of the works of God takes on a new meaning, even urgency. What have we done to God's created world—turning it into a life-threatening place?" [49]

The natural world of our planet is threatened by over-population and global climate change. The combined voices of climatologists, environmental scientists, world leaders, politicians, farmers, nature lovers, youth, and victims of natural disasters spell crisis. At an International Climate Conference in 2018, David Attenborough, respected naturalist and author, warned that climate change threatened "a man-made disaster of global scale", adding that "the collapse of our civilizations and the extinction of much of the natural world is on the horizon." [50] Even our diet may have consequences for global warming. David Suzuki claims that meat consumption is a significant contributor to the problem. Livestock

---

49 Niels-Erik Andreasen, "A Sabbath Rest for the Whole Earth." *Adventist Review*, August 29, 1996, 20.
50 David Attenborough, at a UN Climate Summit, December 2018. https://www.adamwalanus.pl/cytaty.html

production occupies 30 percent of the planet's land surface and is responsible for 18 percent of greenhouse gases such as methane and nitrous oxide. [51]

As stewards of God's creation, we have messed up. However, the committed Christian sees the earth and wildlife as God's creation, and wants to cooperate with him in restoring ecological harmony to our planet. A belief in God as creator, redeemer, and restorer motivates us to find a solution to the environmental crisis. By contrast, "secular ideologies can only motivate people to respect nature and its resources out of fear: fear of punishment or of annihilation if environmental laws are disregarded. . . . It is only when a person understands himself and the world as the object of God's creation and redemption that he will be both convinced and compelled to act as God's steward of his body as well as of the created order. The Sabbath can play a vital role to help in recovering these spiritual values needed to solve the ecological crisis."[52]

God's ancient provision of a sabbath rest for the land that we occupy and work reveals a God who is deeply concerned with what we do with it. We are called to be stewards of our environment, called to counteract the ignorance and greed that sees the earth's resources only as economic opportunity. Sabbath of the seventh day takes us back to a moment in time when God gifted a brand new planet to humanity "to work it and take care of it" (Gen 2:15 NIV). We have failed in that assignment, but one day God will restore the earth to its pristine perfection. Isaiah poetically pictures it this way:

> "The wolf will live with the lamb, the leopard will lie down with the goat, the calf and the lion and yearling together; and a little child will lead them. The cow will feed with the bear, their young will lie down together, and the lion will eat straw like the ox. Infants will play near the hole of the cobra; young children will put their hands into the viper's nest. They

---

51 "Livestock a major threat to environment" FAO Newsroom. http://www.fao.org/NEWSROOM/en/news/2006/1000448/index.html
52 Samuele Bacchiocchi, *Divine Rest for Human Restlessness*. (Berrien Springs, MI: Biblical Perspectives, 1988), 205.

will neither harm nor destroy on all my holy mountain, for the earth will be filled with the knowledge of the Lord as the waters cover the sea (Isa 11:6-9 TNIV)."

My Takeaway: *Sabbath charges me to care for the earth and its creatures.*

Your Takeaway?

A DAY FOR REDEMPTION

Now that you have been freed from sin
and enslaved to God,
the advantage you get is sanctification.
The end is eternal life.
(Romans 6:22 [author's paraphrase])

9

THE COVENANT

It is easy to overlook the second time when the Ten Commandments were given to the Israelites. It happened forty years after the events at Sinai, when a new generation arrived at the borders of their Promised Land. At that time Moses led his people in a review of their past experiences, with re-emphasis on God's Law. Many of the new generation had not personally experienced the marvelous rescue from Egyptian bondage. As Moses publicly read again God's Ten Commandments, his reading of the fourth was startlingly different. Listen:

"Observe the Sabbath day, to keep it holy, as the Lord your God commanded you. Six days you shall labor and do all your work, but the seventh day is the Sabbath of the Lord your God." That part is familiar, and the text continues with the same provision of rest for family members, servants, foreigners, and work animals. But then the wording changes. Instead of giving the six days of creation as justification for observing the seventh day, Moses gives a different reason with these words: *"And remember that you were a slave in the land of Egypt, and the Lord your God brought you out from there by a mighty hand and by an outstretched arm; therefore the Lord your God commanded you to keep the Sabbath day"* (Deut 5:12-15 NKJV).

Had God changed his mind? No, because creation is a theme throughout the ancient Scriptures. In fact, we now have three solid reasons for celebrating the Sabbath—it is a day of *rest* from the work and stress of a week, a time to celebrate our *relationship* to the divine creator and his handiwork, and now, a day to celebrate our *rescue* from the bondage of sin and evil. Sabbath is meant to remind us that we are redeemed, brought back into a relationship with God.

Sign and Covenant

During Israel's encampment at Sinai, God told Moses to instruct the people: "The Israelites are to observe the Sabbath, celebrating it for the generations to come *as a lasting covenant. It will be a sign between me and the Israelites forever,* for in six days the Lord made the heavens and the earth, and on the seventh day he abstained from work and rested" (Exod 31:16,17 TNIV). What does this mean?

To begin, let us talk about covenant. We understand covenant as a signed agreement between two or more parties. The Bible has a lot to say about covenants; the word occurs twenty-five times in the Book of Genesis alone, yet we do not always understand its spiritual meaning for Israel and us. David Asscherick summarizes the entire Bible with three words, in this sequence: *Creation, Conflict,* and *Covenant*.[53]

- *Creation.* Genesis chapters one and two.
- *Conflict.* Genesis chapter three describes the beginning of conflict as Adam and Eve take fruit from a forbidden tree.
- *Covenant.* Genesis 3:15 pries open God's plan to rescue humanity and eventually end the conflict with
- *Creation* again in the last two chapters of the Bible (Rev 21 and 22).

The divine covenant is a contract initiated by God as a response to the "conflict" that began in Eden. It originated as an incredible plan to bring reconciliation and restoration if or when humanity chose to abandon their creator. The plan involved both *relationship* and *redemption. Relationship* meant restoring the intimacy between God and humanity as it was before sin destroyed it. *Redemption* meant rescuing humanity from sin and eternal death.

---

53 David Asscherick, *What is the Bible? God?* Episode 1, Hope Channel, 2013.

The covenant plan is presented as having been made even before creation; it is the story of a "Lamb slain from the foundation of the world" (Rev 13:8 NKJV). No wonder it is named throughout Scripture as an "everlasting covenant."

The word "covenant" is not used in the first three chapters of Genesis, but centuries later, when Israel made the same bad choices, God told them, "Like Adam, you broke my covenant and betrayed my trust" (Hosea 6:7 NLT).

Over time, God introduced his "everlasting covenant" in specific ways to individuals. To Noah after the flood, it signaled a restored creation with assurance of protection and a rainbow as the covenant sign (Gen 9:6-13). To Abraham, it was a promise that he would father "a great nation", with circumcision as his sign, (Gen 12:2, 17:10-13) plus an assurance that his descendants would inherit the land of Canaan (Gen 17:7,8). Ultimately we, his spiritual descendants, are promised an eternal inheritance: "And if you belong to Christ, then you are Abraham's descendants, heirs according to the promise" (Gal 3:29 NASB).

God introduced his covenant to the Israelites soon after he rescued them from Egypt. "You yourselves have seen what I did to Egypt, and how I carried you on eagles' wings and brought you to myself. Now if you obey me fully and keep my covenant, then out of all nations *you will be my treasured possession*" (Exod 19:4,5 NIV). Notice that God's covenant is always about *relationship* and *redemption.*

Throughout the Old Testament we see a God who never abandons his covenant, no matter how much or how often his people fail to respond with loyalty and obedience. On the day that Moses delivered two tablets of stone inscribed by God on Mount Sinai, he challenged his people: "And now, Israel, what does the Lord your God require of you? He requires only that you fear the Lord your God, and live in a way that pleases him, and love him and serve him with all your heart and soul." Moses added, "And you must always obey the Lord's commands and decrees that I am giving you today *for your own good*" (Deut 10:12,13 NLT).

Was the obedience requirement unreasonable? Sigve Tonstad responds: "God restores the people to freedom, self-respect, and dignity, delivering them from slavery in Egypt. . . . God brings them 'out of the house of bondage' for their own sake. Crucially, the values of the Ten Commandments are not the price they have to pay for benefits received. Rather, the commandments embody qualities that will safeguard life and liberty."[54]

God's everlasting covenant is bold and generous. It is loaded with promises and guarantees salvation to every person who accepts Jesus as his savior. It is God's character of love in action : "God loved the world so much that he gave his one and only Son, so that everyone who believes in him will not perish but have eternal life" (John 3:16 NLT).

Through Israel's history, we see a God who is desperate to save eternally the people he rescued from slavery, in spite of their repeated failures. "Oh, that my people would listen to me! Oh, that Israel would follow me, walking in my paths" (Psalm 81:13 NLT)! "They have refused to listen to me and are worshipping other gods. Israel and Judah have both broken the covenant I made with their ancestors" (Jer 11:10 NLT). It was a trail of broken promises, yet God was always ready to forgive and forget their mistakes. Through those times, God used lots of carrots, but sometimes had to wield a stick. "I will discipline you, but with justice; I cannot let you go unpunished" (Jer 46:28 NLT).

We too were born into slavery of sin, but it does not have to stay that way. Writing to Christians in Rome, Paul explained, "I am using the illustration of slavery to help you understand all this. . . . When you were slaves to sin, you were free from the obligation to do right. . . . But now you are free from the power of sin and have become slaves of God. Now you do those things that lead to holiness and result in eternal life. For the wages of sin is death, but the free gift of God is eternal life through Christ Jesus our Lord" (Rom 6:19-23 NLT). God's covenant spells freedom through Jesus!

---

54 Sigve Tonstad, The Lost Meaning of the Seventh Day. (Berrien Springs, MI: Andrews Univ. Press, 2009), 100.

SABBATH AS THE COVENANT SIGN

God introduced the Ten Commandments with this statement: "I am the Lord your God, who brought you out of Egypt, out of the land of slavery" (Exod 20:2 TNIV). That single act was the basis for his covenant with Israel. Within the law, God identified the Sabbath as his covenant sign: "*The Sabbath is a sign of the covenant between me and you*" (Exod 31:13 NLT). You will notice that the fourth commandment affirms God's authority as maker of "the heavens, the earth, the sea, and everything in them" (Exod 20:11 NLT). Sabbath is the given *sign* of the everlasting covenant; Sabbath and Covenant are bound together by *relationship and redemption.*

While the ancient rite of circumcision was part of God's covenant with Abraham and later with Israel, it was Sabbath that became the *eternal* sign of God's everlasting covenant (Exod 31:12,13,17; Ezek 20:12,20).[55] The coming of Jesus was a radical event that brought termination to two Old Testament covenant practices—circumcision and animal sacrifices—but his death introduced two new ones. *Baptism* replaced circumcision: "Your sinful nature was put off when you were circumcised by Christ, having been buried with him in baptism" (Col 2:11,12 TNIV). The *Lord's Supper* replaced the animal sacrifices: "[Jesus] took the cup after supper, saying, 'This cup is the *new covenant* in My blood, which is shed for you'" (Luke 22:20 NKJV).

The "new covenant", as it is frequently called, was predicted by Jeremiah, but later elaborated in the New Testament by the author of Hebrews, who references Jeremiah: "The Holy Spirit also testifies that this is so. For he says, 'This is the new covenant I will make with my people on that day, says the Lord: I will put my laws in their hearts, and I will write them on their minds.' Then he says,

---

55 A *sign* in Scripture is almost always something visible. Circumcision was visible only in an unclothed male, so the female half of the population was excluded. The Sabbath, on the other hand, was instituted at Creation for all time and all people. The Sabbath commandment is inclusive of everyone, male and female—all who celebrate their redemption in Jesus. Sabbath is thus the covenant sign for all time.

'I will never again remember their sins and lawless deeds.' And when sins have been forgiven, there is no need to offer any more sacrifices" (Heb 10: 15-18 NLT, Jer 31:31-34).

Like Israel of old, we are a rescued people. Although we still wander through a wilderness of trouble and temptation, God will never abandon us. "My covenant of blessing will never be broken" (Isa 54:10 NLT). As we journey toward an eternal kingdom, the Sabbath hovers above us as the perpetual sign of God's everlasting covenant for our salvation and a restored relationship with Him.

My Takeaway: *Sabbath is the sign of God's everlasting covenant of love and salvation.*

Your Takeaway?

10

THE PROMISE

The aged warrior gathered his people around him as they stood ready to occupy the promised land. "*Remember,*" Moses said, "that you were once slaves in Egypt, but the Lord your God brought you out with his strong hand and powerful arm. That is why the Lord your God has commanded you to rest on the Sabbath day" (Deut 5:15 NLT).

Did they remember? As the centuries rolled around, prophets had to repeatedly remind Israel of their miraculous deliverance from slavery, but their Sabbath-keeping became more about obeying the law than expressing gratitude for their freedom. "When will the Sabbath be over so we can bring out wheat to sell?" they complained (Amos 8:5 NCV). Keeping Sabbath became a tiresome chore, a repetitive ritual, a missed opportunity to harvest their wealth. "They disregard my Sabbath days so that I am dishonored among them," cried the prophet Ezekiel. "Even common people oppress the poor, rob the needy, and deprive foreigners of justice" (Ezek 22:26,27 TNIV). A day for giving too easily becomes a day for getting.

Failure to keep God's covenant of obedience and social justice led eventually to the destruction of Jerusalem by King Nebuchadnezzar, followed by seventy years of exile in far-away Babylon. The warnings had gone unheeded. When the period of captivity ended, it was a new generation that returned to their ancestral home and took up the task of rebuilding their city.

The home-coming brought hope for a revival of covenant obedience and godliness. In a rebuilt Jerusalem, Nehemiah called everyone together in the city square for a renewal of spiritual commitment. Ezra the scribe brought the Book of the Law (most likely, Deuteronomy) to the assembly. Levite scholars read it aloud "and clearly explained the meaning of what was being read, helping the people understand each passage" (Neh 8:8 NLT). It was a sobering and emotional experience for the listeners. They came together again the following day for a communal commitment. After rehearsing their long history and recalling the rescue from Egypt, the entire congregation made written commitments, including this one: "If the people of the land should bring any merchandize or grain to be sold on the Sabbath or on any other holy day, we will refuse to buy it" (Neh 10:31 NLT). The intentions were genuine.

Did they keep the commitment? When Nehemiah returned to Jerusalem a few years later, he described what he saw. "In those days I saw men of Judah treading out their winepresses on the Sabbath. They were also bringing in grain, loading it on donkeys, and bringing their wine, grapes, figs, and all sorts of produce to Jerusalem to sell on the Sabbath" (Neh 13:15). Nehemiah confronted them and instructed that the gates of Jerusalem be shut as darkness fell every Friday evening. All of this happened during the fifth century B.C.

Five hundred years later, though, when Jesus walked the trails of Palestine, we find a startlingly different picture of Sabbath-keeping. The Jews were now fastidious in their observance of God's holy day. Jesus never had to remind the Jewish people about the importance of Sabbath-keeping. A heap of rules now governed how the day should be observed.

What brought about the change? The edict of King Cyrus permitting return of the exiles came with a stipulation that the Jewish monarchy must not be restored. The people could not have a king. Deprived of royal authority, the temple priesthood soon took a leadership role. Scribes and sages became rabbis who taught the Mosaic Law or Torah. Pharisees emerged as a party of law custodians, developing a complex set of rules for Sabbath observance. The Sanhedrin came into existence as an assembly of watchful elders. The Jews would never again disregard the Sabbath.

A Day for Joy

There was a downside though. The post-exilic Jews articulated their identity as a unique race, a people "chosen" by God for a covenant relationship. Outsiders were excluded from that relationship. Sabbath was for Jews alone. They overlooked what God had said through the prophet Isaiah: "Blessed are those who honor my Sabbath days. Don't let foreigners who commit themselves to the Lord say, 'The Lord will never let me be part of his people'" (Isa 56:2,3 NLT).

A Coming Messiah

"Remember that you were slaves in Egypt" (Deut 5:15 TNIV). The Jews were encouraged to look in two opposite directions—backward to the rescue from Egypt; and forward to a Messiah who would bring release from the bondage of sin. The Old Testament Scriptures count dozens of prophecies about his coming. One of the most compelling came in a vision to the prophet Daniel.

Daniel was among hundreds of young men taken to Babylon at the beginning of the Judean exile. He remembered Jeremiah's prediction of seventy years of captivity for his people (Jer 25:11), and eagerly awaited its end. However, as one monarch after another passed from the scene and the empire of Babylon crumbled and fell to Persia, Daniel began to have anxious thoughts.

So we find Daniel praying one of the longest prayers in the Bible (Dan 9:4-19). Uppermost in his mind was restoration of his beloved Jerusalem and its temple. He recalled God's thundering message at Sinai, warning of consequences if Israel failed to keep his covenant. "We have sinned and done wrong," he cried. "We have been wicked and have rebelled; we have turned away from your commands and laws" (Dan 9:5 TNIV). His heart ached for restoration as he pleaded, "Now, our God, hear the prayers and petitions of your servant. For your sake, Lord, look with favor on your desolate sanctuary" (Dan 9:19 TNIV).

In response, the angel Gabriel came to the prophet with multiple assurances. Yes, there would be a speedy end to the Babylonian exile, and yes, Jerusalem and the temple would soon be rebuilt. Beyond that, however, the long-awaited Messiah would arrive at a specified time. "From the time the word goes out to restore and rebuild Jerusalem until the Anointed One comes" there would be 490 years—notice, ten Jubilee cycles (Dan 9:25 TNIV).[56] The edict of King Cyrus came in 457 B.C. In 27 A.D., Jesus received the anointing of the Holy Spirit at his baptism (Luke 3:21,22). Three-and-a-half-years later, he died on Calvary's cross as the world's Redeemer.

A KINSMAN-REDEEMER

To "redeem", according to the dictionary, is to regain possession of something in exchange for payment. The biblical meaning had its origin in Israel's Jubilee. We saw that the Jubilee—every 49th year—brought *freedom for the poor* through forgiveness of debts, *release* from bondage, and *restitution* of property. If, because of poverty, you had to sell your ancestral land, a male relative could buy it back for you (Lev 25:25). He became your "kinsman-redeemer". The word in Hebrew is *go-el*. A beautiful example is seen in the story of the two widows Naomi and Ruth, recorded in the Book of Ruth. Boaz, a land-owner and relative of Naomi, secured a future for the two women by marrying Ruth, thus becoming their "kinsman-redeemer." The married couple became great-grandparents of King David and progenitors of Jesus.

Now observe what happened when Jesus commenced his ministry. Entering the synagogue at his hometown, Nazareth, on a Sabbath morning, he was given the scroll of the prophet Isaiah, from which he publicly read these words: "*The Spirit of the Lord is on me, because he has anointed me to proclaim good news to the poor. He has sent me to proclaim freedom for the prisoners and recovery of*

---

56 Daniel 9:25-26 reads "there will be seven 'sevens' [49 years] and sixty-two 'sevens' [434 years]. . . After the sixty-two 'sevens', the Anointed One will be put to death" (Dan 9:25,26 TNIV).The Hebrew words of Daniel 9:25-27 have a chiastic structure in which two topics are interwoven—the rebuilding of Jerusalem, and the coming of Messiah.

sight for the blind, to set the oppressed free, to proclaim the year of the Lord's favor" (Luke 4:18,19 TNIV; Isa 61:1,2). The listeners understood this as a Jubilee message.

So, all eyes were on Jesus as he said, "Today this Scripture is fulfilled in your hearing" (Luke 4:21 TNIV). Jesus was making his mission statement. He was proclaiming that he had come to bring good news for the poor, release from sin's servitude, and wholeness to humanity. He would sacrifice himself to buy back our lost freedom. He had come as the world's "Kinsman-Redeemer."

The long-awaited promise had reached its fulfillment. Messiah had come, a Redeemer who would deliver from the scourge of evil that had engulfed the planet. His mission would bring release and rejoicing. When Paul cried out, "Who will release me from this life that is dominated by sin and death?" he was able to answer his own question: "Thank God! The answer is in Jesus Christ our Lord!" (Rom 7:24,25 NLT)

My Takeaway: *Sabbath celebrates my rescue from the bondage of sin.*

Your Takeaway ?

11

THE FULFILLMENT

The Jewish people should have recognized Jesus as the on-time fulfillment of dozens of prophetic promises from their Scriptures. They should have seen his coming as the longed-for consummation and culmination of all their sacrifices, sabbaticals, and jubilees. His mission coincided with one grand meaning of the Sabbath—a deliverance from servitude and a restitution of social justice. It should have reminded them of their long past deliverance from Egyptian bondage, the more recent release from Babylonian exile, and now, "freedom for the prisoners" of Satan—the breaking of chains that held all humanity captive. Unfortunately, with myopic vision, they saw only their immediate craving for deliverance from the oppression of Rome.

Even John the Baptist, chosen to announce Christ's arrival, misunderstood the nature of his mission. Languishing in Herod's dungeon, John sent two of his disciples to ask Jesus, "Are you the one who was to come, or should we expect someone else?" Without answering the question, Jesus told them to "go back and report to John what you hear and see. *The blind receive sight, the lame walk, those who have leprosy are cleansed, the deaf hear, the dead are raised, and the good news is proclaimed to the poor*" (Matt 11:2-5 TNIV). Jesus was fulfilling his mission statement.

Jesus had a special interest in everything he had created, including the meticulously designed and fine-tuned human body. Sin had long since marred its perfection, bringing disease, wasting, blindness, and terminal illness. Wherever he turned, Jesus saw twisted bodies and sick minds, and he longed to bring wholeness and restoration. His heart of love yearned to repair the brokenness and bring release from pain. No surprise, then, that the divine Creator spent more of his time healing and restoring than in teaching and preaching.

"The Blind Receive Sight"

A young man with sightless eyes sits begging in one of Jerusalem's crowded alleys.[57] As Jesus comes by, his disciples ask him a question: "Why was this man born blind? Was it because of his own sins or his parents' sins?" The question does not surprise Jesus, because Jews commonly believed that sickness resulted from a sinful act.

"It was not because of his sins or his parents' sins," Jesus replies. "This happened so the power of God could be seen in him." That said, he spits on the ground, makes some mud with saliva, and pastes it over the man's eyes. "Go wash yourself in the Pool of Siloam."

We may react with shock or disgust. We expected Jesus would simply touch the man's eyes, or say, "be made to see" and witness the amazement of onlookers. Instead, the young man does not see who is bending over him, and now has to find someone to help him get all the way down to the Siloam pool near the Kidron valley. It requires robust faith and obedience, but the man perseveres and comes home seeing. "I went to Siloam and washed, and now I can see!" he exclaims to an excited circle of his parents and friends.

Not everybody is happy, however, because this day is Sabbath. Jesus has broken multiple Sabbath laws which include preparing a medicine for healing. Some Pharisees discover what Jesus has done and announce, "This man Jesus is not from God, for he is working on the Sabbath." All day they harass the healed man and his parents. He argues courageously that only one sent from God could have given him sight. Exasperated, he quizzes his interrogators, "Do you want to become his disciples too?" Angrily, they throw him out of

---

57 Read John 9:1-41.

the synagogue with insults: "You were steeped in sin at birth. How dare you lecture us!"

Then Jesus finds him. "Do you believe in the Son of Man?" he asks. "Who is he, sir?" the man implores. "I want to believe in him." Jesus responds, "You have seen him, and he is speaking to you." Looking up at the face of Jesus, the young man exclaims, "Yes Lord, I believe!" and falls down in worship.

Who were the blind ones in this story? Spiritual blindness is a malady with serious outcomes. Jesus, Lord of the Sabbath, still works to open blind eyes. And the cure still demands faith and obedience.

"THE LAME WALK"

Another day in Jerusalem.[58] Jesus passes the large Bethesda Pool near the Sheep Gate. All around the pool are disabled people with a variety of infirmities. It is commonly believed that an angel sometimes stirs the water, offering healing to the first person who enters. Among the invalids is a man who has been paralyzed for thirty-eight years. Jesus addresses him: "Would you like to get well?" The man, not knowing the questioner, shrugs hopelessly: "Sir, I have no one to help me into the pool when the water is stirred."

Forget about the pool. Jesus is speaking. "Get up! Pick up your mat, and walk!" Did the man hear correctly? It's impossible, of course, but with a surge of faith the crippled man stands, rolls up his sleeping mat and begins walking, as in a dream, for the first time in thirty-eight years!

"Now the day on which this took place was a Sabbath." Uh-oh! If you want to attract attention in Jerusalem on a Sabbath day, you carry your sleeping mat through the streets. Soon religious leaders stop him: "You can't work on the Sabbath! The law doesn't allow you to carry that sleeping mat!" When they discover he has just received healing, there is double trouble. You can rescue your

---

58 Read John 5:1-18; 7:19-24.

donkey if he falls into a pit on Sabbath, but healing a man is against the rules.

All through Sabbath, the Jewish leaders harass Jesus. "My Father is always working, and so am I," Jesus tells them. This Rabbi claims God as his Father! What blasphemy! "For this reason they tried all the more to kill Him."

The confrontation continues. These Pharisees uphold the Law of Moses, which includes instruction that circumcision be performed on the eighth day after birth (Exod 12:43-49). Jesus accosts them: "Moses gave you the Law, but none of you obeys it! In fact, you are trying to kill me. I did one miracle on the Sabbath and you were amazed. But you work on the Sabbath, too, when you obey Moses' law of circumcision. If the correct time for circumcising your son falls on the Sabbath, you go ahead and do it so as not to break the Law of Moses. So why should you be angry with me for healing a man on the Sabbath" (John 7:19-23 NLT)?

The Bible has no record of anyone asking Jesus to heal him on a Sabbath. They knew better. Jesus took the initiative in all his Sabbath healings, and always chose situations where the person had been infirmed for a long time. He could have postponed these healings until after sundown or to a following day; but his Sabbath healings were intentional. He wanted to show that Sabbath and wholeness are interconnected. He wanted to free the day for healing and joy.

HEALING AND SALVATION

He came with two significant names, both recorded by Matthew. *Immanuel*—*"God with us"*—speaks of a restored *relationship* (Matt 1:23; Isa 7:14). The other name was given by an angel to Joseph: "You are to give him the name *Jesus*, because he will *save* his people from their sins" (Matt 1:21 TNIV). He is also our *Redeemer*.

To accomplish his mission, Jesus, the God-Man, lived on earth as one of us. "It was necessary for him to be made in every respect like us, his brothers and sisters, so that he could be our merciful

A Day for Joy

and faithful High Priest before God" (Heb 2:17 NLT). In Jubilee parlance, he became our *go-el*, our Kinsman-Redeemer.

Each Sabbath prompts us to remember what Jesus accomplished for us on Calvary. He gave us back what we lost through sin. Jesus Christ, our nearest of kin, had the prerogative and compassion to pay the price of our lost inheritance and redeem us. Paul the apostle confirms it. When the right time came, he says, God sent his Son who became our Kinsman-Redeemer by adopting us into his family. "God sent him to buy freedom for us who were slaves to the law, so that he could adopt us as his very own children. And since you are his child, God has made you his heir" (Gal 4:5,7 NLT).

Faith is required to accept forgiveness and healing. For the Israelites preparing to leave Egypt, it meant wiping blood on their door posts. For the man born blind, faith meant going to Siloam to wash. For the paralytic, faith meant obeying a seemingly impossible instruction to get up and walk. For you and me, faith is believing that Christ's death on Calvary will make us clean. Ellen White confirms: "If you believe the promise—believe that you are forgiven and cleansed—God supplies the fact. You are made whole, just as Christ gave the paralytic power to walk when the man believed that he was healed. It *is* so if you believe it." [59]

Jesus' ministry involved more than physical healing of bodies and minds. It was also about forgiveness and salvation. John Brunt shows that a Greek word sometimes translated "made well" in the gospel accounts may also be translated as "saved." Several times when Jesus healed someone, he sent them home, saying, "Your faith has made you well" (Matt 9:22; Mark 10:52; Luke 17:19). His words might just as well have been, "Your faith has *saved* you." [60] The physical healing designated his power to save and make whole.

It was not a coincidence that the two healings in Jerusalem took place on Sabbath days. "The Sabbath receives its meaning because it symbolizes salvation, and in it we can participate in the

---

59 Ellen White, *Steps to Christ*. (Washington: Review and Herald, 1908), 51.
60 John C. Brunt, *A Day for Healing*. (Nampa, ID: Pacific Press, 2016), 25.

wholeness provided by Christ through faith. Jesus uses the Sabbath as a means to save life and to bring healing and wholeness through fellowship with Him. . . Jesus Christ and salvation stand at the heart of the Sabbath."[61]

My Takeaway: *Sabbath is about healing and wholeness.*

Your Takeaway ?

---

61 Brunt, 68.

RECESSION

Guard yourselves and God's people.
I know that false teachers,
like vicious wolves,
will come in among you after I leave,
not sparing the flock.
Even some men
from your own group
will rise up and distort the truth
in order to draw a following.
Watch out!
(Acts 20:28-30 NLT)

12

SABBATH IN RECESSION

Christians commonly believe that Sabbath of the seventh day was given only for the Israelite community. I have tried to show that the Old Testament evidence is otherwise. God always sought to extend his covenant blessings beyond the Israelite nation. Even as the nation went into decline and exile, God had plans for the salvation of Gentiles and continuity of the Sabbath.[62] Speaking through Isaiah: "Don't let foreigners who commit themselves to the Lord say, 'The Lord will never let me be part of his people'. I will also bless the foreigners who commit themselves to the Lord, who serve him and love his name, who worship him and do not desecrate the Sabbath day of rest, and who hold fast to my covenant." God added, "My Temple will be called a house of prayer for all nations" (Isa 56:3,6,7 NLT).

Undeniably, Jesus came as an agent of change. His topsy-turvy kingdom upset all the boundaries that defined "outsiders" in Jewish society—Gentiles, Samaritans, tax-collectors, the poor, the uneducated, the sick and maimed, lepers, the blind, the demonized, women in general but especially widows, and anyone else who ignored Jewish rituals. Jesus taught and practiced equality of all persons. He deplored a religion that emphasized external piety but lacked compassion. His ministry demonstrated that love was law in action.

Throughout his ministry, Jesus taught the purpose of his coming and revealed a God of love and compassion. He preached no new doctrine, but broadened the meaning of several old ones.

---

62 Sigve Tonstad, *The Lost Meaning of the Seventh Day*. (Berrien Springs, MI: Andrews Univ. Press, 2009), 148.

"You shall not murder" included thoughts of anger and hate (Matt 5:21,22). "You shall not commit adultery" included lust (Matt 5:27,28). The Sabbath was more about healing and joy than attendance at worship, though Jesus himself was consistent in synagogue attendance (Luke 4:16).

Emphasizing his role as creator, Jesus proclaimed himself as "Lord, even of the Sabbath" (Mark 2:27,28). He had made the Sabbath as a holy gift for people, not for Jews alone, and he sought to free the day from a tangled heap of regulations that crippled its impact on society. He redefined Sabbath as a day of healing and joy. I find not a shred of evidence that he planned for annulment or change to any of the Ten Commandments, including the Sabbath commandment. Indeed, when he predicted the future destruction of Jerusalem, he urged the faithful to pray "that your flight will not take place in winter or on the Sabbath" (Matt 24:20 TNIV).

It is apparent that Paul, apostle to the Gentiles, observed Sabbath throughout his ministry, "as was his custom" (Acts 17:2), but he had insight into some religious trends that were already in evidence before his death (Acts 20:28-30). Paul was present at a conference of early Christian leaders when they hotly debated whether Gentile Christians should be required to practice circumcision (Acts 15). Can you imagine how a whispered thought of abolishing or changing the weekly day of worship would have generated a tsunami through the early Christian community?

Luke was traveling with Paul when the apostle first visited Macedonia. There was no Jewish synagogue at Philippi, so Luke tells how on Sabbath Paul and his companions went outside the city to find a small group of believers at the riverside (Acts 16:13-15). Sabbath appears to have been consistently observed through New Testament times. There is no biblical evidence that Sabbath was annulled or supplanted during the time of the apostles.[63]

---

63 Some see a new emphasis when the apostle John was in vision on Patmos on "the Lord's Day" (Rev 1:10). Was this Sunday? In parts of Asia Minor, where John spent much of his life as teacher and evangelist, the first day of each month was celebrated as the Emperor's Day. Some believe

A Day for Joy

Isn't it strange, then, that most of the Christian world today does not worship on the seventh day? At some point in time, the seventh day was lost or forgotten by the Christian community. How did it happen?

THE EARLY CHURCH AND JEWISHNESS

In the middle years of the first century, there was a change in public attitudes toward Jews and their religion. Jews were mostly tolerated by the Romans until the time of the Great Jewish Revolt around A.D. 66. The Zealots, a fanatical and powerful faction in Judea, incited violence against Rome until A.D. 70, when the Roman army plundered Jerusalem and destroyed its temple. The Zealots were crushed, but the aftermath was distrust and animosity toward Jews and their religious practices. Christians in Jerusalem followed Jesus' advice and fled to the small city of Pella in the mountainous region east of Galilee.[64] (Matt 24:20)

A second Jewish rebellion occurred in 135 A.D. Like the Zealot uprising, it was ruthlessly crushed by Rome, and like the earlier revolt, it had devastating consequences for Jews and Jewish-Christians alike. Harsh restrictions were imposed on Jews throughout the Empire. Christians everywhere were suspect and sometimes persecuted for their observance of the "Jewish" Scriptures, including Sabbath. Under those circumstances, it was inevitable that church leadership would fall to Gentile Christians, who tended to distance themselves from anything perceived to be Jewish.

We know little about development of the Church in the period between the two Jewish rebellions of 70 A.D. and 135 A.D. One church historian writes, "For fifty years after St. Paul's life, a curtain hangs over the church, through which we vainly strive to look; and when at last the curtain rises, about A.D. 120, with the writings

---

that a day of the week was also called the "Lord's Day" in deference to the Emperor. Thus, by referencing the Lord's Day, John may have been making a direct challenge to emperor worship, as he does elsewhere in his book. (*NIV Cultural Backgrounds Study Bible*, note on Revelation 1:10).

64 "Flight to Pella." Wikipedia article.

of the earliest Church Fathers, we find a church in many respects very different from that in the days of St. Peter and St. Paul." [65]

After the two Jewish rebellions there was fear among Gentile Christians of being branded as Jews. We see this in the writings of Ignatius, one of the Apostolic Fathers,[66] in the early part of the second century. Ignatius was Bishop of Antioch in Syria, the city where followers of Christ were first called "Christians" (Acts 11:26). In one of his letters, Ignatius advised his parishioners to "no longer keep the Sabbath after the Jewish manner, and rejoice in days of idleness . . . but let every one of you keep the Sabbath after a spiritual manner, rejoicing in meditation of the law." [67] But he followed that counsel with this: "After the observance of the Sabbath, let every friend of Christ keep the Lord's Day as a festival, the resurrection-day, the queen and chief of all the days."

In his letter, Ignatius mentioned the "resurrection day." It is easy to overlook the importance of the resurrection to the early Christians, including Jesus' disciples. Everything changed for eleven confused and disillusioned men when an angel at the tomb declared, "He is not here; he has risen, just as he said" (Matt 28:6 TNIV). That event ignited them for a ministry that changed the world. Peter declared, "God has raised this Jesus to life, and we are all witnesses of the fact" (Acts 2:32 TNIV). Paul affirmed, "Christ has indeed been raised from the dead. . . . Death has been swallowed up in victory" (1 Cor 15:20,54 TNIV)! The Book of Acts overflows with stories of the gospel's rapid expansion all over the Roman world, in spite of Greek philosophy that discredited the idea of bodily resurrection (Acts 17:31,32). [68]

---

65 Jesse L. Hurlbut, *The Story of the Christian Church*. (Grand Rapids, MI: Zondervan, 1967), 41.
66 The Apostolic Fathers were early theologians who are believed to have known some of the Twelve Apostles or St. Paul.
67 "Epistle of Ignatius to the Magnesians." Quoted by Gary Hullquist in *Sabbath Diagnosis*. (Brushton, NY: Teach Services, 2004), 108. (Also, Ante-Nicene Christian Library, v.1).
68 Luke, the writer of Acts, was a Greek and a Gentile by birth. He twice references "the first day of the week." Once was at Troas in Asia Minor,

A Day for Joy

Confusion and uncertainty about which day to worship is evident during the first four centuries of the Christian Church. It is reported, for example, that Ambrose, Bishop of Milan, kept Sabbath with his congregation while in Milan, and Sunday when he was in Rome.[69] Writers such as Irenaeus (the Bishop of Lyons) and Clement of Alexandria, attempted to re-interpret Scripture to harmonize with religious practices.[70] Their writings remind us of Peter's warning about those who would "distort the Scriptures to their own destruction" (2 Peter 3:16 NASB).

Writing about the middle of the second century, Justin Martyr, a young Greek philosopher who converted to Christianity, described worship thus: "On the day called Sunday, all who live in cities or in the country gather together to one place and the memoirs of the apostles or the writings of the prophets are read, as long as time permits. . . . Then we all rise together and pray, and, when our prayer is ended, bread and wine and water are brought. . . . Sunday is the day on which we hold our common assembly, because it is the first day on which God, having wrought a change in the darkness and matter, made the world; and Jesus Christ our Savior on the same day rose from the dead." [71]

A fourth century manuscript from Antioch, purporting to reflect early liturgical practices, has this instruction: "You must fast on the day of the Preparation, because on that day the Lord suffered the death of the cross under Pontius Pilate. But keep the Sabbath

---

when Paul celebrated communion with new believers until midnight on Sunday because his ship sailed for Macedonia next morning (Acts 20:7). When Paul wrote to believers at Corinth, he admonished them to put aside money each Sunday morning to meet the needs of poor believers, as he had also instructed the Galatians to do (1 Cor 16:1-2). It is apparent that Troas, Corinth, and Galatia were mainly Gentile congregations.

69 Gary Hullquist, *Sabbath Diagnosis*, 117.
70 Kenneth A. Strand, "Tertullian and the Sabbath" in *Andrews University Seminary Studies*, 9 (1971), 129-146.
71 "First Apology of Justin Martyr" (Ante-Nicene Christian Library, v.2), 65,66.

and the Lord's day festival; because the former is the memorial of the creation, and the latter of the resurrection."[72]

As Christianity became a Gentile church, it was easy for converts to transfer their allegiance from pagan gods to the worship of the resurrected Christ on the day that traditionally venerated the Sun god. Why associate their worship practice with Judaism, a despised sect that denied the Christ and held religious ceremonies on the seventh day, the one honoring Saturn? In the fourth century, Emperor Constantine embraced Christianity and declared Sunday as the day of worship. In reality, he was confirming by statute what was already a widely accepted practice.

But what about the long-established purposes of Sabbath worship? Could worship on any other day of the week usurp the multiple meanings of seventh-day worship? Sigve Tonstad puts the question this way: "When the Sabbath goes into eclipse, it is necessary to ask questions like the following: What happened to its portfolio of meaning? Did Sunday assume the massive portfolio? Could the meanings hitherto invested in the Sabbath realistically be outsourced to another entity?"[73] How could first-day worship usurp the Sabbath view of the earth and the human creation?

Faithful Sabbath-Keepers

The power of the church at Rome grew with support of the Emperors. Soon after the Christian canon of the Scriptures was affirmed by the church in 393 A.D., the circulation and reading of the Scriptures was strictly controlled. Despite the threat of persecution for unauthorized distribution of the Word of God, there were pockets of resistance. In the rugged mountains of northern Italy, isolated communities of Waldenses cherished the Scriptures and some of them paid with their lives. Groups of Albigenses in southern France met a similar fate.

---

72 "Apostolic Constitutions", book 7, section ii, paragraph xxiii. (Ante-Nicene Christian Library, v.24)
73 Tonstad, 298

A Day for Joy

Not all Christian believers discarded the Sabbath. In the eastern part of the Empire—Syria, Egypt, and Ethiopia—communities continued to cherish and faithfully observe the seventh-day.[74] There is documentary evidence that as late as the 16th century there were isolated pockets of Sabbath-keepers in Russia, Poland, Germany, and Austria. In Ireland and Scotland, branches of the Celtic Church observed the seventh-day from earliest times until at least the 11th century, and Sabbath-keeping was practiced in scattered areas of England and Wales through the 17th century. [75] Tonstad quotes this congregational prayer from a group of fourth-century Syriac Christians:

"Lord, almighty, you created the world through Christ, and set apart the Sabbath to remember this; because on it you rested from your works, for meditation on your laws. . . . You gave them the Law of ten oracles, clearly expressed by your voice and written by your hand. You commanded them to keep the Sabbath. . . . For the Sabbath is rest from creation, the completion of the world, the seeking of laws, the thankful praise to God for those things which were given to men."[76]

Protestant reformers of the 16th century released the Scriptures from the chokehold of the medieval church, but missed the opportunity to free the Sabbath from its bondage. Philip Melanchthon, a colleague of Martin Luther, acknowledged the power of the Roman Church when he wrote, "They refer to the Sabbath Day as having been changed into the Lord's Day, contrary to the Decalogue, as it

---

74 Charles E. Bradford, *Sabbath Roots: the African Connection*. (Barre, VT: Brown & Sons Printing Inc., 1999). Also Kenneth A. Strand, "A Note on the Sabbath in Coptic Sources" in *Andrews University Seminary Studies*, 6 (1968), 150-157.

75 Samuele Bacchiocchi, *Divine Rest for Human Restlessness*. (Berrien Springs, MI: Biblical Perspectives, 1988), 51-53. Bryan W. Ball, *The Seventh-Day Men: Sabbatarians and Sabbatarianism in England and Wales, 1600-1800*. (London: Oxford Univ. Press, 1994). J.N. Andrews, *History of the Sabbath and First Day of the Week*. 2nd ed. (Battle Creek, MI: Steam Press of the Seventh-day Adventist Publishing Association, 1873), chapters 21 and 24.

76 Tonstad, 3,4

seems. . . . Great, say they, is the power of the Church, since it has dispensed with one of the Ten Commandments."[77]

My Takeaway: *The Seventh Day was consistently kept by Jesus and the Apostles*

Your Takeaway?

---

77 Quoted by Philip Schaff, *The Creeds of Christendom*, vol.3. (London: Harper, 1878), 64.

13
CREATION IN PAIN

Addressing Christians in Rome, Paul wrote, "The creation looks forward to the day when it will join God's children in glorious freedom from death and decay. For we know that all creation has been groaning as in the pains of childbirth right up to the present time. And we believers also groan , even though we have the Holy Spirit within us as a foretaste of future glory, for we long for our bodies to be released from sin and suffering" (Rom 8:21-23 NLT). What did Paul mean by those words? Were creation and bodies in trouble?

Paul was writing at a momentous time. The Empire of Rome held sway in the political realm, but the prevailing culture of thought and art emanated from the earlier sovereignty of Greece. In the time of Jesus and the apostles, the Hebrew Scriptures were already available in a Greek translation known as the Septuagint.

The core elements of Greek philosophy originated with Plato, who lived three centuries before Christ. Plato conceived the idea of dualism, with a separate existence for body and soul. In Plato's thinking, the soul was naturally and innately immortal. It belonged to the world of the divine, but was forced to inhabit a body, which it despised.

Greek dualism was the almost invisible, yet accepted worldview in the time of Paul. Its influence was pervasive and persuasive. Its emphasis on the separation of the soul from the body presented a challenge to the beliefs of the Christian church. Make every effort to purify the soul. The body will perish and burn in everlasting hell, so deprive and punish it. "This view led to a diminished interest in nature because concern for the body brings no apparent spiritual benefit. The body is only the prison of the soul; why explore it? Life in this world is brief compared to eternity; why bother to understand it? The earth has no place in God's ultimate reality; why study it?"[78]

When we remove Sabbath from Creation, detaching it from God's completed work of forming the earth and humanity, we lose the meaning of our natural world and even of ourselves. We saw this happen when Philo, a Jew of Alexandria, tried to re-cast the Old Testament scriptures in the context of Platonic philosophy. In his re-interpretation of the Old Testament, he saw a dis-connect between creation and the Sabbath.[79]

Dualism and Christian Thought

The Scriptures do not support Plato's concept of a separate body and soul. God made humans as whole beings (Gen 2:7). The Bible knows nothing of an immortal soul distinct from the body. That belief came into Christianity from Hellenistic philosophy after the time of Christ and the apostles.[80] The Bible overflows with

---

78 Sigve Tonstad, *The Lost Meaning of the Seventh Day*, 331.
79 Herold Weiss, *A Day of Gladness: the Sabbath among Jews and Christians in Antiquity*. (Columbia, SC: Univ. of South Carolina Press, 2003).
80 Some statements from Christian writers:
Gerrit C. Berkouwer: "It appears clearly, then, that Scripture never pictures man as a dualistic, or pluralistic being. . . . There can be no idea of an essential dualism in Paul." (*Man: The Image of God.* Grand Rapids, MI: Eerdmans, 1962, 203, 207).
George Eldon Ladd: "Fundamental to Hebrew thought is the belief that God is the creator, that the world is God's creation and is therefore in itself good. The Greek idea that the material world is the sphere of evil and a burden or a hindrance to the soul is alien to the Old Testament." (*The Pattern of New Testament Truth.* Grand Rapids, MI; Eerdmans, 1968, 28).
Clark Pinnock: "Anthropological dualism . . . has fostered many false dichotomies including a negative view of the body in contrast to the soul and a concept of salvation as interior experience rather than total transformation." ("The Conditional View" in *Four Views on Hell*, edited by William Crockett. Grand Rapids, MI: Zondervan, 1996, 149).

A Day for Joy

images of creation from the first verse of Genesis to the last chapter of Revelation. David exclaimed, "The heavens declare the glory of God; the skies proclaim the work of his hands" (Psalm 19:1 TNIV). The Sabbath revels in that magnificence and calls us to celebrate by worshipping our Creator. "You are worthy, our Lord and God, to receive glory and honor and power, for you created all things" (Rev 4:11 TNIV).

The pinnacle of creation was the making of the first man and woman. "You made all the delicate, inner parts of my body," exclaimed King David. "Thank you for making me so wonderfully complex" (Psalm 139:13,14 NLT)! It seemed to David that every part of his body carried an invisible stamp: "Designed by God."

The first act of sin was to destroy the sacredness of the earth and the body. The human race spiraled downwards into a ruptured and fractured society. In one of Jesus' parables, some field workers asked the farmer why weeds had appeared with his planted corn. The farmer shook his head: "An enemy did this," he said. (Matt 13:27,28).

In the first century of the Christian church, Hellenistic philosophy was already tainting the pure message of the gospel. It introduced weeds of asceticism and dualism—separation of soul and body—into the soil of Christian thinking. Belief in an immortal soul led to estrangement from the material world. Suddenly the earth and the body were suspect, and the seventh day lost part of its meaning.

PUNISHING THE BODY

"Man's duty is to free himself from the chains of the body in which the soul lies fast bound like the prisoner in his cell." [81] Silently

---

N. T. Wright: "God will rescue the entire creation from corruption and decay. . . . He will give all his people new bodies, like Jesus' risen body, to live gloriously within his new world." (*Paul for Everyone: Romans, part 1.* Louisville, KY: Westminster John Knox Press, 2004, 12).

81 Erwin Rohde, *Psyche: The Cult of Souls and the Belief in Immortality Among the Greeks.* (London: Routledge, 1925), 342.

and stealthily, Greek dualism infiltrated the Christian Church. The concept of an immortal soul and a perishing body found its way into Christian thinking. The human body was considered perishable and punishable.

Peter Harris asks, "Is Christianity a Body-Hating Worldview?" Answering his own question, he writes, "The Bible celebrates the value of the body as God's creation and as an integral part of a unified concept of human being. In the first account of creation in Genesis, humanity is described in exalted terms as being created in the image of God."[82]

That is not the way many medieval Christians saw themselves. Following are accounts of some Christian saints and monks in the early and medieval centuries:[83]

- ❖ Origen of Alexandria (3rd century) was one of the Church Fathers, a scholar and theologian: "God made the present world and bound the soul to the body as a punishment. It appears that even the use of bodies will cease, and if this happens, bodily nature returns to non-existence." Demetrius accused Origen of castrating himself to purify his soul.

- ❖ Simeon Stylites (5th century) was an ascetic saint who deprived himself by living for 37 years on a platform on top of a pillar near Aleppo, Syria.[84]

- ❖ Pier Damiani (11th century) was a Benedictine monk and a cardinal in the circle of Pope Leo IX. Damiani introduced a practice of severe flagellation at his monastery. "Flagellate

---

82 Peter Harris, "Is Christianity a Body-Hating Worldview?" https://www.bethinking.org/is-religion-harmful/is-christianity-a-body-hating-worldview.

83 Unless otherwise indicated, these statements are taken from "Asceticism – Western Asceticism – The Middle Ages."
   http://science.jrank.org/8388/Asceticism-Western-Asceticism-Middle-Ages.html

84 "Simeon Stylites." Wikipedia article.

oneself for the duration of forty psalms daily; one-half times more on holy days."

- ❖ Bartholomew of Farne (12th century) was a Benedictine hermit in England. "We must inflict our body with all kinds of adversity if we want to deliver it to perfect purity of the soul."

- ❖ St. Francis of Assisi (13th century) occasionally dreamed that demons were tormenting him. On one such occasion, he cried, "In the name of Almighty God, you demons, do all that is within your power to my body, do your worst. I will willingly endure it all, because I have no greater enemy than my body, and when you vent your fury on it, you will be doing me a service and avenging me on my adversary."[85]

- ❖ Saint Dominic (13th century) was a Spanish priest and the founder of the Dominican Order. It is recorded that "three times every night he would whip himself with an iron chain: once for himself, once for the sinners in the world, and once for the sinners who are suffering in purgatory."[86]

Infliction of "adversity" on the body during the dark years of the medieval church included fasting almost to death, self-scourging, and mutilation. The body was disposable. During long centuries, disinterest in the body and its functioning led to abysmal ignorance, filth, disease, and premature death for ordinary people. By the fourteenth century, conditions were ripe for a terrible calamity known as the Black Death or bubonic plague. The pandemic swept across Europe, decimating one third of its population. By mid-century, 24 million people had died from the plague, described as "the most lethal disaster of recorded history."[87] The disease was carried by rats, but no one seemed to be aware of that. When a fleet of ships

---

85 Recorded by Jacobus de Varagine in *The Golden Legend*.
86 Timeline of the Life of St. Dominic. http://opeast.org/2014/08/timeline-of-the-life-of-st-dominic
87 Barbara W. Tuchman, *A Distant Mirror: The Calamitous 14th Century*. (New York: Knopf, 1928).

arrived at the port of Messina, Italy, in October 1347, the fearful port authorities prevented the crew from coming ashore, but not the rats and fleas.[88]

By sowing the wind, humanity was reaping the whirlwind. Some words of the prophet Jeremiah depict the agony of a creation in turmoil:

> "I looked at the earth, and it was formless and empty;
> And at the heavens, and their light was gone.
> I looked at the mountains, and they were quaking;
>
> All the hills were swaying.
> I looked, and there were no people;
> Every bird in the sky had flown away"
> (Jer 4:23-26 TNIV).

Recovery from the medical wilderness that gripped the western world for nearly two millennia was painfully slow. As late as the middle of the nineteenth century, medical practice could not be called "medical science" by today's standards. Blood-letting was a common treatment, strychnine and arsenic were prescribed to cure ailments, medical staff saw no need to wash their hands before and during surgeries, and Louis Pasteur had yet to demonstrate his germ theory. British soldiers who fought in the Crimean War in 1855 died in large numbers—not from their battle wounds, but from diseases caused by filthy conditions in army hospitals. Knowledge of health and hygiene was 3,500 years behind the health practices and wisdom of Moses and the wandering Israelites.

The author of James White's biography tells how the Whites and a staff of a dozen helpers pioneered in publishing the Adventist church paper at Rochester, New York, in the early 1850's. All were young people, most of them in their twenties, but "young as they may seem today, in a century when life expectancy was only in the

---

88 Tonstad, 332, 333.

40s, half or more of their lives were already over. Indeed, four of them would soon be dead."⁸⁹

My Takeaway: *When we detach Sabbath from Creation, both lose meaning.*

Your Takeaway?

---

89 Gerald Wheeler, *James White, Innovator and Overcomer.* (Hagerstown, MD: Review and Herald, 2003), 73.

RESTORATION

And I saw another angel
flying through the sky,
carrying the eternal Good News
to proclaim
to the people who belong
to this world—
to every nation, tribe,
language, and people.
"Fear God," he shouted,
"Give glory to him.
For the time has come
when he will sit as judge.
Worship him who made the heavens,
the earth, the sea,
and all the springs of water."
(Revelation 14:6,7 NLT)

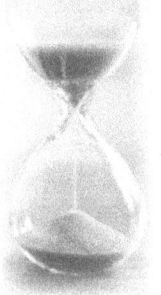

14

SABBATH RESTORATION

Knowledge of the seventh-day Sabbath came to the United States of America with some Seventh Day Baptists from England. Believers there had worshipped on the seventh day in isolated communities since the early 1600s. Arriving in America, some of them established the first Sabbatarian meeting house at Newport, Rhode Island, in 1729.[90]

Scroll down to the middle years of the nineteenth century where, in America, there was widespread expectation that Christ's second coming would take place in October of 1844. It became known as the Millerite movement, named for William Miller who originated it. Early in the same year, a Seventh Day Baptist named Rachel Oaks visited at a small country church in rural New Hampshire. The preacher that Sunday was a circuit-riding Methodist minister named Frederick Wheeler. After the sermon, Oaks challenged Wheeler to obey *all* of God's commandments, including the fourth. Wheeler listened, studied the Bible for himself, and became a Sabbath-keeper. His preaching likely influenced a Baptist friend, Thomas Preble, to keep the seventh day. In 1845, Preble published a tract advocating its observance.[91]

When Christ did not appear in October 1844 there was catastrophic disappointment among thousands of Christian believers in New England and other parts of America. One of the disappointed was a retired sea captain named Joseph Bates, living in the New Bedford area of Massachusetts. The failure of Jesus to appear

---
90 "Seventh Day Baptists" Wikipedia Article.
91 George R. Knight, *A Brief History of Seventh-day Adventists*. (Hagerstown, MD: Review & Herald, 2012).

brought him first, confusion, but then a deeper study of the Bible. He read Preble's tract and made a trip to New Hampshire to visit with Frederick Wheeler before accepting the Sabbath in 1845. Bates shared his discovery with some Millerite friends, among them James and Ellen White. These three had a formative influence in the founding of the Seventh-day Adventist Church in 1863.[92]

Sabbath Calling

Seventh-day Adventists sounded an apocalyptic call from the Book of Revelation to re-instate a biblical worldview. An angel "flying in mid-air" was seen to have "the eternal gospel to proclaim to those who live on the earth—to every nation, tribe, language and people." His message in a loud voice was a clarion call to spread this message: "Fear God and give him glory, because the hour of his judgment has come. *Worship him who made the heavens, the earth, the sea, and the springs of water*" (Rev 14:6,7 TNIV). Referencing those words of the fourth commandment, it was an end-time call to worship the Creator of the earth, the Maker of humankind, and Lord of the Sabbath. It was a call to re-engage with the God of creation. It led Seventh-day Adventists to observe and promote the Sabbath of creation. They also took ownership in promoting health and wholeness for the body, defending its sacredness from an emerging belief that it evolved.

A new interest in health made its appearance in mid-nineteenth century America. While physicians and scientists struggled to find their way out of the medical wilderness that had gripped the western world for nearly two thousand years, a health-reform movement was born in the United States. Seventh-day Adventists became known and respected for their emphasis on healthful living, teaching that the human body reflects God's image and should be viewed as sacred.

In contrast, Charles Darwin's evolutionary theory, first published in 1859, presented a direct challenge to Christians who held

---

[92] Knight, *Joseph Bates, the Real Founder of Seventh-day Adventism*. (Hagerstown, MD: Review & Herald, 2004).

belief in God, creation, and the sacredness of the body. William Provine, a professor of biological sciences at Cornell University, painted this dismal picture of humanity during a debate at Stanford University in 1994: "Let me summarize my views on what modern evolutionary biology tells us loud and clear, and I must say that these are basically Darwin's views. There are no gods, no purposeful forces of any kind, no life after death. . . . There is no ultimate foundation for ethics, no ultimate meaning in life, and no free will for humans, either."[93]

Our 21st century world world is perplexed by many things. We are pressured by neocapitalism which builds an obsession to work harder and acquire more things. The loss of spiritual identity with a creator leads to a sense of lostness, purposeless living, and a turning to alcohol, drugs, and sex; all to fill an emptiness that can be filled only by identifying with something beyond ourselves. Timothy Johnson, a nationally respected physician, writes: "Virtually all religions and mythologies share a common sense that human beings are in relationship to someone or something suprahuman. This sense is heightened by indications from brain researchers that we are, in casual terms, 'hard-wired for God'."[94]

As our world's problems pile up, where shall we turn for answers? Meaninglessness and loss of hope draw young and old to death as a way out. Sabbath speaks to these tragic losses. Identity with a divine creation gives meaning to life, and redemption from sin brings assurance and hope.

Forty years ago, Marva Dawn portrayed a society drifting without a moral code: "Increasingly in our culture, the Ten Commandments do not provide the moral foundation for society. The commandment to worship God and him only was the first to be lost, but now, to a tragic extent, our culture no longer respects the

---

93 "Darwinism: Science or Naturalistic Philosophy?" [VHS Tape]. The Debate at Stanford University between William B. Provine and Philipp E. Johnson, 1994.

94 Timothy Johnson, *Finding God in the Questions*. (Downers Grove, IL: IVP Books, 2006), 67.

commands to honor parents and not to commit adultery. Many people wonder how these outdated commandments can matter in a twentieth-century world. In fact, the commandments as a clear basis for morality are desperately needed more than ever in our fragmented, disrespectful, violent, and covetous society. It seems to me that to recover the command to keep the Sabbath might help our Christian communities to restore the other commandments."[95]

We are called back to the all-embracing biblical Sabbath. Sigve Tonstad writes: "The roots of the Sabbath are sunk in the original soil of the divine-human relationship, enriched and nourished afresh by the encounters and visions of patriarchs and prophets who grasped God's purpose. . . . The need for belonging, the necessity of rest, and the encounter with something larger than oneself all find expression in the blessing of the seventh day. The Sabbath roots of our common humanity are beckoning all to join in the final homecoming."[96]

My Takeaway: *Sabbath responds to an end-time call to worship the Creator.*

Your Takeaway ?

---

95 Marva J. Dawn, *Keeping the Sabbath Wholly*. (Grand Rapids, MI: Eerdmans, 1989), 43.
96 Sigve Tonstad, *The Lost Meaning of the Seventh Day*. (Berrien Springs, MI: Andrews University Press, 2009), 504, 505.

15

SABBATH-KEEPING

How do you "keep" Sabbath? What occupies your time on that day? We are back to the question I put at the beginning of my Introduction to this book: "What does Sabbath mean to you?" In fourteen short chapters we have explored the meaning and personal import of the seventh day. Which brings this final question: How should I observe Sabbath as it comes to me each week?

We spend most of our lives in the things of space. We live in space, and we work to gain space— we buy space, rent space, negotiate our entitlement to space, steal space and fight over its ownership. Abraham Heschel writes, "Six days a week we wrestle with the world, wringing a profit from the earth. . . . Space is exposed to our will; we may shape and change the things in space as we please." In contrast, he says, "Time is beyond our reach, beyond our power." [97] Within the realm of time we are all equal—no one has more or less of it due to power or position.

Sabbath belongs to the realm of time. "Sabbath is the day that bridges two great events in time: the creation by God and the re-creation of the new heavens and earth by God."[98] Sabbath is a weekly reminder that God is sovereign and life has meaning.

---

[97] Abraham Heschel, *The Sabbath, its meaning for modern man*. (New York: Farrar, Strauss, 2005) 13, 99.

[98] Dan B. Allender, *Sabbath*. (Nashville, TN: Thomas Nelson, 2009), 49, 56

SABBATH TIME

So, what shall we do with Sabbath, this holy time? When Joseph Bates introduced Sabbath to early Adventist believers in America, he emphasized law above faith as the way to salvation. "His legalistic tendencies, his confusion between behavior and religion, and his living in the fear of judgment perspective did not have a healthy influence on later Seventh-day Adventism."[99] Sabbath-keeping as obedience rather than love response to a Redeemer has characterized several generations of Seventh-day Adventists. One church leader who sought to change the emphasis was William W. Prescott, who in 1893 asked and answered this question: "What then is Sabbath-keeping? It is the sign to the Christian that his hope, his confidence, are entirely in Jesus Christ, who is the Creator and Redeemer."[100]

John Brunt identifies two different ways of relating to Sabbath—two mind-sets. One is the "rules mind-set" where we try to obey by determining what we should *not* do during Sabbath hours. It is a misguided attempt to protect the Sabbath by building a fence around it, like the Pharisees did in Jesus' time. The joy of the Sabbath is lost, along with its meaning in an age of spiritual confusion.[101]

There is a better way. It is what Brunt calls the "relational mind-set." We put Jesus at the center, so the question is not 'Have I kept the rules?' but 'Have I entered into fellowship with Christ so that I experience his presence in my life, healing me, opening my eyes, and making me whole?'"[102] Experiencing Jesus as my friend and savior will not make me less careful in my Sabbath observance. "He is a Person who seeks a close, one-on-one relationship with

---

99 George Knight, *Joseph Bates, the Real Founder of Seventh-day Adventism*. (Hagerstown, MD: Review and Herald, 2004), 212.
100 William W. Prescott, *Christ and the Sabbath*. (Washington: International Religious Liberty Association, 1893), 22.
101 John C. Brunt, *A Day for Healing*. (Nampa, ID: Pacific Press, 2016), 73..
102 *Ibid.*, 74

A Day for Joy

you and me. God does not want us to merely believe in him. He wants to relate to us on a personal level."[103]

There are many ways to use Sabbath time unselfishly and to God's glory. How I spend Sabbath will have something to do with my age, family relationships, physical location, need for bodily rest, and so on. But whatever I do, the Sabbath hours should bring me peace and joy. God promises, "Enjoy the Sabbath and speak of it with delight as the Lord's holy day. Honor the Sabbath in everything you do on that day, and don't follow your own desires or talk idly. Then the Lord will be your delight" (Isa 58:13,14 NLT). Let us look at some options for spending Sabbath hours.

- **Welcoming Sabbath**. The seventh day begins at sundown on Friday and ends at sundown on Saturday. How should I prepare for and experience its arrival? Making my home clean and tasteful is conducive to restfulness. Susannah Heschel describes how her family welcomed Sabbath with lighting of candles at sunset on Friday: "My mother and I kindled the lights for the Sabbath, and all of a sudden, I felt transformed, emotionally and even physically."[104]

  When I was a boy, our family of four gathered in the living room on Friday evening. Dad and my brother played favorite hymns on their violins, with me on piano; then we knelt in a circle for prayers. Much later, with children of our own, we sometimes met at my brother's house to welcome Sabbath, followed by a meal of soup and freshly baked buns. We also marked close of Sabbath with worship.

- **Corporate Worship**. We commonly associate Sabbath-keeping with morning attendance at church, where we worship our maker with music and singing, prayer, study of the Word, and sharing testimonies of God's love and care. It does not have to happen in buildings dedicated for that purpose. Early Christians met together in homes (Acts 2:46,47). We are urged

---

103 Henry and Richard Blackaby, *Experiencing God*. (Nashville, TN: B&H Publishing, 2008), 2.
104 Susannah Heschel, in Abraham Heschel. *The Sabbath*, vii, xiii.

to "not give up meeting together, as some are in the habit of doing" (Heb 10:25 TNIV). Corporate worship, wherever it happens, should be a time of joy. "Come, let us sing for joy to the Lord. Let us come before him with thanksgiving and extol him with music and song. Come, let us bow down in worship" (Psalm 95:1-6 TNIV).

- **Time for Family**. On weekdays family members are scattered in different directions to work and school, with hurried meals and "after hours" trajectories to sports, music lessons, professional meetings, internet, or television. Sabbath brings family togetherness as we give time to God and each other. It is a day for belonging and relationship.
- **Time with Jesus**. The busyness of six days necessarily limits the time we spend with the Word, but the seventh is prime time to connect with the Lord of the Sabbath. Children are drawn to Jesus not only through the Gospel accounts but from stories all across the Bible. Teens as well as adults may recapture the passion, humor, and beauty of Scripture from contemporary paraphrases.[105]
- **Time for Community**. Sabbath is a time for community, for inclusiveness, for sharing the joy and the good news of salvation through Jesus. Enjoy a meal with friends, stroll together in a park or through the woods, share life stories, spend time with someone who needs a friend. It is good to be free from the slavery of clocks and schedules. Jesus set a beautiful example in the way he shared Sabbath time with his followers, often using opportunities to bring healing to the sick. "To relieve the afflicted, to comfort the sorrowing, is a labor of love that does honor to God's holy day."[106]

Sabbath ought to be a sanctuary for the lonely and isolated. It "affirms the place for every person in God's family—the

---

[105] The *Voice Bible* is adaptable for group participation in reading Bible stories. *The Voice Bible: Step into the Story of Scripture*, by Ecclesia Bible Society. (Nashville, TN: Thomas Nelson, 2012).
[106] Ellen White, *The Faith I Live By*, 36.

resident alien, the immigrant mother, the Korean family that lives next door, the Latino teenager, the man dying of AIDS, the women of all races who know domestic violence, all of society's marginalized. The Sabbath is a sanctuary for the alien, a sanctuary where there is always room for another person, because it is a place in time, not space."[107]

- **Time with Nature**. "If the Sabbath sends us anywhere, it is to nature."[108] Since the beginning of earth time, Sabbath has been inseparable from creation, and though the earth is sadly diminished by sin, there is yet much to inspire. God's love of variety is seen in every facet of his handiwork. Prepare to be surprised and delighted by his wisdom and creativity. Children love the wild and wonderful in nature. If you spend most of your life at a desk, climbing a mountain may bring wonder and exhilaration. Dan Allender describes a snorkeling experience in the Caribbean, where "God's love of variety is on parade around every reef. It is as if God splashed the canvas to see what would happen to the image when color and shape are bent in new ways."[109]

- **Time for Quiet**. Sabbath may also bring the blessing of silence. "If there is a time and place for us to hear the voice of God, it is in the midst of quiet."[110] Confined by a world of noise and distraction, we have largely forgotten the meaning of solitude, reading God's Word, and prayerful meditation. "Be still and know that I am God" (Psalm 46:10). We have the example of Jesus: "Very early in the morning, while it was still dark, Jesus got up, left the house and went off to a solitary place, where he prayed" (Mark 1:35 TNIV). Sabbath peace is an opportunity to mend our tattered lives.

---

107 Kendra Haloviak, "The Sabbath Song." *Adventist Review*, August 29, 1996, 35.
108 Allender, 66.
109 *Ibid.*, 84.
110 *Ibid.*, 166.

The world's religions build great cathedrals or temples, but Sabbath wraps holiness in time. "As we keep the Sabbath, instead of our possessing things or space, time possesses us."[111] We celebrate creation and redemption and anticipate a wonderful homecoming. When the Jews came home from the long captivity in Babylon, priests led the people in a special celebration: "You alone are the Lord. You made the heavens, even the highest heavens, and all their starry host, the earth and all that is on it, the seas and all that is in them. You give life to everything, and the multitudes of heaven worship you" (Neh 9:6 TNIV).

I conclude this chapter with these words from Marva Dawn: "In an age that has lost its soul, Sabbath keeping offers the possibility of gaining it back. In an age desperately searching for meaning, Sabbath keeping offers a new hope. In contrast to the technological society, in which the sole criterion of value is the measurement of efficiency, those who keep the Sabbath find their criteria in the character of God, in whose image they celebrate life."[112]

My Takeaway: *Sabbath wraps holiness in time.*

Your Takeaway?

---

111 Marva J. Dawn, *Keeping the Sabbath Wholly*. (Grand Rapids, MI: Eerdmans, 1989), 40.
112 *Ibid.*, 50.

16

HOME-COMING

There were two phases—two separate events—in the redemption of Israel. The first part—their rescue from Pharaoh and slavery—was an incredible event, but it left them homeless. For forty years they wandered around in the wild lands of Sinai and the Palestinian Negev. There were rough times during those desert wanderings, but God pitched his tent with them and kept alive his promise of a new and permanent home. Liberation from bondage had been the first part of his plan. The other part—phase two—was settlement in their "promised land" (Exod 6:8).

A home-coming awaits us too. The prophet Isaiah, living in the days of King Hezekiah, peered ahead to a coming return from Babylonian exile, but also beyond to a new earth. "The Lord's redeemed come home; they shall enter Zion with shouts of triumph, crowned with everlasting gladness. Gladness and joy shall be their escort, and suffering and weariness shall flee away" (Isa 35:10 NEB).

In vision, the apostle John witnessed two amazing scenes of worship around God's throne. In the first, he watched as "twenty-four elders" laid their crowns before the throne and joined their voices, exclaiming, "You are worthy, our Lord and God, to receive glory and honor and power, *for you created all things, and by your will they were created and have their being*" (Rev 4:11 TNIV). In the second scene, he saw "a Lamb, looking as if it had been slain" which brought forth this song: "You are worthy to take the scroll and to open its seals, *because you were slain, and with your blood you purchased for God members of every tribe and language and people and nation*" (Rev 5:9,10 TNIV). Humanity's creation and redemption are the source and songs of worship in heaven.

King David recorded "A Song to be Sung on the Sabbath Day." We may join him in these words of his song:

> "It is good to give thanks to the Lord,
> > to sing praises to the Most High.
> It is good to proclaim
> > your unfailing love in the morning,
> Your faithfulness in the evening,
> To the music of the ten-stringed lyre
> > and the melody of the harp.
> You thrill me, Lord, with all you have done for me!
> I sing for joy because of what you have done"
> > (Psalm 92:1-4 NLT).

John the Apostle brings the creation-redemption story to finality in the last two chapters of the Bible. Taking some words from Isaiah, he writes with wonder: "Then I saw 'a new heaven and a new earth', for the first heaven and the first earth had passed away. . . . And I heard a loud voice from the throne saying, 'Look! God's dwelling place is now among the people, and he will dwell with them. They will be his people, and God himself will be with them and be their God" (Rev 21:1,3 TNIV). "Month by month at the new moon, week by week on the Sabbath, all mankind shall come to bow down before me, says the Lord" (Isa 66:23 NEB).

My Takeaway: *Sabbath Joy is forever!*

Your Takeaway?

MY TAKEAWAYS

Jesus affirmed Sabbath as a time to share joy and kindness (chapter 1)

God instituted the Seventh Day as the memorial of his creation (chapter 2)

Sabbath is a day of rest after six days of work and stress (chapter 3)

Sabbath impacts my outlook and behavior through the entire week (chapter 4)

Sabbath calls me to care for people in desperate need (chapter 5)

Sabbath tells me who I am and why I'm here (chapter 6)

Sabbath challenges me to keep my body and mind clean and healthy (chapter 7)

Sabbath charges me to care for the earth and its creatures (chapter 8)

Sabbath is the sign of God's everlasting covenant of love and salvation (chapter 9)

Sabbath celebrates my rescue from the bondage of sin (chapter 10)

Sabbath is about healing and wholeness (chapter 11)

The Seventh Day was consistently kept by Jesus and the Apostles (chapter 12)

When we detach Sabbath from Creation, both lose meaning (chapter 13)

Sabbath responds to an end-time call to worship the Creator (chapter 14)

Sabbath wraps holiness in time (chapter 15)

Sabbath Joy is forever! (chapter 16)

Sabbath: A Select Bibliography

Allender, Dan B., *Sabbath*. (Nashville, TN: Thomas Nelson, 2009).

Andreasen, Niels-Erik, *The Christian Use of Time*. (Nashville, TN: Abingdon Press, 1978).

Rest and Redemption: A Study of the Biblical Sabbath. (Berrien Springs, MI: Andrews University Press, 1978).

Andrews, John Nevins, *History of the Sabbath and First Day of the Week*. 2nd edition. (Battle Creek, MI: Steam Press of the Seventh-day Adventist Publishing Association, 1873).

Bacchiocchi, Samuele, *Divine Rest for Human Restlessness: A Theological Study of the Good News of the Sabbath for Today*. (Rome: Pontifical Gregorian University Press, 1980).

Ball, Bryan W., *The Seventh-day Men: Sabbatarians and Sabbatarianism in England and Wales, 1600-1800*. (London: Oxford University Press, 1994).

Bradford, Charles E., *Sabbath Roots: The African Connection*. (Barre, VT: Brown & Sons, 1999).

Brueggemann, Walter, *Sabbath as Resistance: Saying No to the Culture of Now*. (Louisville, KY: Westminster John Knox Press, 2017).

Brunt, John C., *A Day for Healing*. (Nampa, ID: Pacific Press, 2016).

Davidson, Jo Ann, *Rediscovering the Glory of the Sabbath*. (Nampa, ID: Pacific Press, 2020)

Dawn, Marva J., *Keeping the Sabbath Whollly*. (Grand Rapids, MI: Eerdmans, 1989).

Heschel, Abraham, *The Sabbath, its Meaning for Modern Man*. (New York: Farrar, Straus, 2005).

Hullquist, Gary, *Sabbath Diagnosis*. (Brushton, NY: Teach Services, 2004).

Knight, George R., *Joseph Bates, the Real Founder of Seventh-day Adventism*. (Hagerstown, MD: Review and Herald, 2004).

Kubo, Sakae, *God Meets Man: A Theology of the Sabbath and Second Advent*. (Nashville, TN: Southern Publishing Association, 1978).

MacCarty. Skip, *In Granite or Ingrained? What the Old and New Covenants Reveal about the Gospel, the Law, and the Sabbath*. Berrien Springs, MI: Andrews Univ. Press, 2007.

Perspectives on the Sabbath; 4 views. Edited by Christopher John Donato. (Nashville, TN: B&H Publishing, 1911).

Prescott, William Warren, *Christ and the Sabbath*. (Washington: International Religious Liberty Association, 1893).

Schroeder, Gerald L., *The Hidden Face of God*. (New York: Simon & Schuster, 2001).

Strand, Kenneth A., *The Early Christian Sabbath: Selected Essays and a Source Collection*. (Ann Arbor, MI: Ann Arbor Publishers, 1979).

"The Sabbath is for Joy": A Special Issue of the *Adventist Review*, August 29, 1996.

Tonstad, Sigve, *The Lost Meaning of the Seventh Day*. (Berrien Springs, MI: Andrews University Press, 2009).

Walton, John H., *The Lost World of Genesis One*. (Downers Grove, IL: IVP Academic, 2009).

Weiss, Herold, *A Day of Gladness: the Sabbath among Jews and Christians in Antiquity*. (Columbia, SC: University of Southern Carolina Press, 2003).

www.ingramcontent.com/pod-product-compliance
Lightning Source LLC
LaVergne TN
LVHW041631070426
835507LV00008B/555